1996
Happy
Birthday,
Willie!

your purr
loving,

best Cats!

Two-Minute
BRIDGE
TIPS

Two-Minute
BRIDGE
TIPS

BY FRANK STEWART

CRESCENT
NEW YORK · AVENEL

ACKNOWLEDGMENTS

The columns contained herein first appeared in "Sheinwold on Bridge" and were copyrighted by the Los Angeles Times Syndicate. The material appears by kind permission of Alfred Sheinwold and the Los Angeles Times Syndicate.

Copyright 1992 by the Los Angeles Times Syndicate and Frank Stewart.

This 1995 edition published by Crescent Books, distributed by Random House Value Publishing, Inc. 40 Engelhard Avenue, Avenel, New Jersey 07001.

Random House
New York • Toronto • London • Sydney • Auckland

A CIP catalog record for this book is available from the Library of Congress.

ISBN 0-517-12318-5

10 9 8 7 6 5 4 3 2 1

DEDICATION

To Nell

PREFACE

I originally wrote the material in this book for the syndicated newspaper column "Sheinwold on Bridge." Since 1986, it has been my honor and pleasure to work with the inimitable Alfred Sheinwold in producing that column.

Column deals are usually "single-problem," meaning that they contain just one point of technique. Newspaper space is too limited for more. (The toughest part of column writing is slicing every ounce of fat from my prose to get down to the proper length.) Mr. Sheinwold insists that our columns contain a play point, though the bidding may be instructive as well. The deals in this book cover the spectrum of technique, and the reader — unless he is a top expert — can expect to see his game improve.

Even if you're a national champion, I hope that *Two-Minute Bridge Tips* will entertain you and enhance the time you spend at the bridge table.

Frank Stewart

Fayette, Alabama
March, 1995

1.

Dlr: East	♠ Q J 10
Vul: None	♥ K J 5
	♦ 6 4 2
	♣ 8 4 3 2

♠ A 9 8 7 4 2
♥ 7 3
♦ A 10 3
♣ A Q

East	South	West	North
Pass	1♠	Pass	2♠
Pass	4♠ (!)	All Pass	

West leads the ♦Q, and East plays the nine. Plan the play.

2.

Dlr: South	♠ J 6
Vul: None	♥ 10 4 2
	♦ A 5 4 3
	♣ A Q 4 2

♠ A Q 8 3
♥ J 7
♦ Q 10 8 2
♣ 8 6 5

```
        N
    W       E
        S
```

South	West	North	East
1♠	Pass	2♣	Pass
2 NT	Pass	3 NT	All Pass

You lead the ♦2: three, nine, jack. South then leads the ♠2. How do you defend?

FRANK STEWART

3.

Dlr: South   ♠ A Q
Vul: N-S   ♥ Q 9 4 2
                 ♦ 7 3
                 ♣ A J 4 3 2

                 ♠ 8
                 ♥ A K J 10 8 3
                 ♦ A 9 4
                 ♣ K 6 5

South	West	North	East
1♥	Pass	3♥	Pass
4♦	Pass	5♥	Pass
6♥	All Pass		

West leads the ♦Q. Plan the play.

4.

Dlr: South   ♠ J 2
Vul: N-S   ♥ A Q 6 2
                 ♦ 8 5
                 ♣ K 7 5 4 2

                 ♠ A K Q 10 6 4 3
                 ♥ 9 4
                 ♦ A J
                 ♣ A 3

South	West	North	East
2♠	Pass	3♣	Pass
3♠	Pass	4♠	Pass
5♣	Pass	5♥	Pass
6♠	All Pass		

West leads the ♥8. Plan the play.

1.

Three Wishes

Once there was a bridge player with a magic bottle, inside which lived a genie who could grant the customary three wishes. Since our hero badly needed a top score in the deal below, he overbid to game. West led the queen of diamonds, and South, on seeing dummy, hastily summoned the genie.

"You called, master?"

"I wish for the trump finesse to work," South requested.

"Done," nodded the genie. "What else?"

"I wish for the club finesse to work."

"Done. And do you also wish to guess right in hearts?"

"Nope," said South. "For my third wish, I wish for three more wishes."

Makes Game

The genie sulkily dematerialized back into the bottle, and South took the ace of diamonds and tried a heart to the *king* at the second trick. (South knew from the opening lead that East had the king of diamonds, and he had to assume that East, a passed hand, held kings in clubs and spades; thus, East couldn't hold an ace.) Declarer next led the queen and jack of spades and continued with a club to the queen. With the black kings well placed, South made his game.

The moral: even if no genie is handy when you must locate a key honor, try making a wish about the position of other honors. Then draw the appropriate conclusions.

BIDDING QUIZ

You hold: ♠ 3 ♥ A 10 8 4 2 ♦ Q J 8 ♣ J 9 7 6. Your partner opens two spades, strong. You respond 2NT, and he next bids three hearts. The opponents pass. What do you say?

ANSWER: Bid five hearts. After partner's strong two-bid, his change of suit is forcing. Since you would raise to four hearts if your ace were a low heart, your actual hand is worth a try for slam. Your hand has great trick-taking power opposite partner's major two-suiter.

Dlr: East
Vul: None

```
                        ♠ Q J 10
                        ♥ K J 5
                        ♦ 6 4 2
                        ♣ 8 4 3 2
      ♠ 3                              ♠ K 6 5
      ♥ A 10 8 4 2                     ♥ Q 9 6
      ♦ Q J 8                          ♦ K 9 7 5
      ♣ J 9 7 6                        ♣ K 10 5
                        ♠ A 9 8 7 4 2
                        ♥ 7 3
                        ♦ A 10 3
                        ♣ A Q
```

East	South	West	North
Pass	1♠	Pass	2♠
Pass	4♠(!)	All Pass	

Opening lead: ♦Q

2.

The Subject Was Rose

At a bridge club on Second Avenue, there haunts the tables a player known to one and all as Secondhand Rose.

Rose suffers from all the woes her famous counterpart in the song had, plus one problem the original Secondhand Rose was spared. The day they taught second-hand play on defense, Rose the bridge player must have been out marrying Jiggs the plumber.

Rose was West in the deal below. South took the jack of diamonds at the first trick and led a low spade toward dummy's jack. True to her name, Secondhand Rose ... with the queen.

Club Shift

Rose shifted to clubs, and declarer played low from dummy. East won the jack and returned a heart to South's ace. South then led another spade. Rose went up with the ace, of course (her play didn't matter at that point), and South had three spade tricks, two hearts, three diamonds and a club.

Rose's defense was second-rate; this time, "second hand low" was a winning guideline. If Rose lets dummy's jack win the first spade, South loses three spade tricks and takes only eight tricks in all.

BIDDING QUIZ

You hold: ♠ K 10 7 5 2 ♥ A K 3 ♦ K J 6 ♣ 10 7. Your partner opens one club, you respond one spade, and he rebids two clubs. The opponents pass. What do you say?

ANSWER: Bid 3NT. Since partner's rebid limited his hand, you must place the contract. Since you have balanced distribution and points in the unbid suits, notrump should be best; you need not try a devious bid of two diamonds, hoping to hear partner support spades.

```
Dlr: South          ♠ J 6
Vul: None           ♥ 10 4 2
                    ♦ A 5 4 3
                    ♣ A Q 4 2
   ♠ A Q 8 3                          ♠ 9 4
   ♥ J 7                              ♥ Q 9 8 6 5
   ♦ Q 10 8 2                         ♦ 9 7
   ♣ 8 6 5                            ♣ K J 9 3
                    ♠ K 10 7 5 2
                    ♥ A K 3
                    ♦ K J 6
                    ♣ 10 7
```

South	West	North	East
1♣	Pass	2♣	Pass
2 NT	Pass	3 NT	All Pass

Opening lead: ♦2

3.

Musical Comedy

"G'luck," said the old music professor as he tabled his dummy for slam in the deal below.

"Don't worry," South replied confidently. "I can Handel it."

South won the ace of diamonds at the first trick and drew trumps. He then took the king of clubs and finessed with the jack. The contract began to un-Ravel when East won the queen and cashed the king of diamonds.

"Bad luck," said South, trying to keep his composer.

"Franck-ly, you gave the slam a Verdi poor try," the professor retorted. "I'll make you a Liszt of books on dummy play."

Duet

"Combine your chances," the prof went on. "It's like playing a duet. Cash the A-K of clubs. If the queen falls, you're home. If both defenders follow low, you're still alive. Finesse with the queen of spades. If it wins, pitch a club on the ace of spades and ruff a club. Dummy has two good clubs for diamond discards, and you actually make seven."

South wanted to go into Haydn. "I'll stop by your office tomorrow after lunch," he said, "to pick up that list."

"Fine," the professor replied. "I'm always Bach by two, Offenbach by one-thirty."

BIDDING QUIZ

You hold: ♠ K 10 7 6 3 ♥ 7 5 ♦ K 8 5 2 ♣ Q 9. Your partner deals and opens 1NT, and the next player passes. What do you say?

ANSWER: Your hand is too strong to sign off with two spades, but too weak to force with three spades. Bid two clubs, Stayman, promising game interest. If partner bids two spades, your hand has improved; raise to four spades. If he bids two diamonds or two hearts, try two spades.

```
Dlr: South          ♠ A Q
Vul: N-S            ♥ Q 9 4 2
                    ♦ 7 3
                    ♣ A J 4 3 2
   ♠ J 9 5 4 2                      ♠ K 10 7 6 3
   ♥ 6                              ♥ 7 5
   ♦ Q J 10 6                       ♦ K 8 5 2
   ♣ 10 8 7                         ♣ Q 9
                    ♠ 8
                    ♥ A K J 10 8 3
                    ♦ A 9 4
                    ♣ K 6 5
```

South	West	North	East
1♥	Pass	3♥	Pass
4♦	Pass	5♥	Pass
6♥	All Pass		

Opening lead: ♦Q

4.

A Devil of a Deal

We know temptation got its start in the Garden of Eden. It should come as no surprise that bridge was involved, particularly since many people swear that the Devil invented the game.

After Lucifer recruited a fourth from the land of Nod, Adam and Eve, sitting North-South, bid to a fine slam. Lucifer, West, led a seductive eight of hearts.

"I can resist anything but temptation," mused Eve, and she finessed with dummy's queen. East (East of Eden?) won the king and returned the jack of hearts to force the ace. Eve then had no chance; with clubs breaking 4-2, she lacked enough entries to set up a long club for the 12th trick.

The Fall

Eve fell from grace at the first trick; she should play a low heart from dummy, letting East win the ten.

If East returns a diamond up to dummy's weakness, Eve wins the ace, takes the A-K of clubs and ruffs a club with a high trump. She then leads a spade to the jack, ruffs a club high, draws trumps and gets back to dummy with the ace of hearts to pitch her diamond loser on the good club.

BIDDING QUIZ

You hold: ♠ J 2 ♥ A Q 6 2 ♦ 8 5 ♣ K 7 5 4 2. Your partner opens one diamond, and the next player passes. What do you say?

ANSWER: Since you have only an average hand, you must limit your strength quickly. You have enough points to bid clubs at the level of two, but not enough to bid hearts next (forcing) if partner rebids two diamonds or 2NT. Thus, let the clubs go and respond one heart to search for a fit in the major.

```
Dlr: South          ♠ J 2
Vul: N-S            ♥ A Q 6 2
                    ♦ 8 5
                    ♣ K 7 5 4 2

♠ 9 5                              ♠ 8 7
♥ 8 7 3                            ♥ K J 10 5
♦ K 9 7 6 3 2                      ♦ Q 10 4
♣ J 6                              ♣ Q 10 9 8
                    ♠ A K Q 10 6 4 3
                    ♥ 9 4
                    ♦ A J
                    ♣ A 3
```

South	West	North	East
2♠	Pass	3♣	Pass
3♠	Pass	4♠	Pass
5♣	Pass	5♥	Pass
6♠	All Pass		

Opening lead: ♥8

5.

Dlr: South
Vul: N-S

       ♠ Q 10 8 5 4
       ♥ 8 6 3
       ♦ A 4
       ♣ 4 3 2

       ♠ A K J 9 6 2
       ♥ A K J
       ♦ K
       ♣ A Q 9

South	West	North	East
2♠	Pass	3♠	Pass
4 NT	Pass	5♦	Pass
5 NT	Pass	6♣	Pass
6♠	All Pass		

West leads the ♦Q. Plan the play.

6.

Dlr: South
Vul: N-S

       ♠ Q 9 6 5
       ♥ A J
       ♦ A 10 9 3
       ♣ A K J

       ♠ A K J 8 4
       ♥ K 10 5 3
       ♦ J 8 2
       ♣ 5

South	West	North	East
1♠	Pass	3♦	Pass
3♠	Pass	6♠	All Pass

West leads the ♣4. Plan the play.

7.

Dlr: South
Vul: N-S

♠ 10 7 4
♥ Q 9 2
♦ Q 5
♣ K Q J 5 3

♠ K J 6 2
♥ A 8
♦ J 10 9 8 7
♣ 7 2

```
    N
 W     E
    S
```

South	West	North	East
1 NT	Pass	3 NT	All Pass

South wins your lead of the ♦J with dummy's queen and leads a heart to his king. How do you defend?

8.

Dlr: South
Vul: N-S

♠ 7 2
♥ 5 4
♦ A K 10 9 5 3
♣ J 8 3

♠ A Q 6
♥ A J 3
♦ Q 2
♣ A 10 9 6 2

South	West	North	East
1 NT	Pass	3 NT	All Pass

West leads the ♣4, and East plays the ten. Plan the play.

5.

Slam Expunged

South in the deal below was an expert, yet he failed to exploit every chance at his slam. He won the first trick, drew trumps and then, as a leading exponent of finesses, found it expedient to lead a heart to his jack.

West took the queen and led another diamond. South threw a club on dummy's ace and led a club to finesse with his queen. When West produced the king, declarer expelled an expletive, and the slam expired for an expensive loss.

Expiation

South sought expiation. "I expected ONE finesse to win," he explained.

North, ready to explode, expressed himself in explicit terms (expurgated here). "Expend more thought," he expounded. "Explore the chance of an end play."

"Cash the A-K of hearts," North expanded, "lead a trump to dummy, discard the jack of hearts on the ace of diamonds, ruff a heart, go back to dummy with a trump and lead a club to the nine. When West wins, he must either return a club into your A-Q or give you a ruff-sluff."

Poor South was thus exposed to all as an ex-expert. Let's hope he at least learned something from the experience.

BIDDING QUIZ

You hold: ♠ 7 ♥ Q 9 4 ♦ Q J 10 6 3 ♣ K 10 6 5. Your partner opens one spade, you respond 1NT, and he rebids two spades. The opponents pass. What do you say?

ANSWER: Pass and hope for a plus. Partner has a minimum hand with a six-card spade suit. If you stretch to bid 2NT, you may be defeated in that contract if partner is weak in hearts or clubs. Worse, he may bid again and land in a hopeless game.

Dlr: South	♠ Q 10 8 5 4		
Vul: N-S	♥ 8 6 3		
	♦ A 4		
	♣ 4 3 2		

♠ 7		♠ 3
♥ Q 9 4		♥ 10 7 5 2
♦ Q J 10 6 3		♦ 9 8 7 5 2
♣ K 10 6 5		♣ J 8 7

	♠ A K J 9 6 2
	♥ A K J
	♦ K
	♣ A Q 9

South	West	North	East
2♠	Pass	3♠	Pass
4 NT	Pass	5♦	Pass
5 NT	Pass	6♣	Pass
6♠	All Pass		

Opening lead: ♦Q

FRANK STEWART

6.

It Might Have Been

What's the perfect deal of bridge? For one player, it's the deceptive play that baffles the opposition. For another, it's 13 top tricks at 7NT. The deal below shows that the game has its abstract beauties.

South took the ace of clubs and drew two rounds of trumps. West discarded, but South still had many chances to make his slam. He chose to cash the top hearts and ruff a heart with the nine of spades. East overruffed and got a diamond trick later.

Double Finesse

"I had no reason to finesse with the jack of hearts," South muttered, "and I also go down if I try the double finesse in diamonds."

"The saddest words of tongue or pen ..." North sighed.

South should simply draw trumps and lead the eight of diamonds for a finesse. When East wins, he is end-played in three suits. Any return gives declarer a 12th trick.

Notice the elegance of the winning play, with each side suit standing ready to provide the slam-fulfilling trick. It would have been a lovely slam to make.

BIDDING QUIZ

You hold: ♠ A K J 8 4 ♥ K 10 5 3 ♦ J 8 2 ♣ 4. You open one spade, and your partner responds two diamonds. The opponents pass. What do you say?

ANSWER: Bid two hearts. Partner could easily have a four-card heart suit, and this is your best chance to locate a fit. To raise diamonds is premature when you have another major suit to show. Nor must you rebid spades to show five; a two-heart rebid will imply at least five spades.

```
Dlr: South        ♠ Q 9 6 5
Vul: N-S          ♥ A J
                  ♦ A 10 9 3
                  ♣ A K J
♠ 2                              ♠ 10 7 3
♥ Q 9 8 6 4                      ♥ 7 2
♦ 7 4                            ♦ K Q 6 5
♣ 10 8 6 4 3                     ♣ Q 9 7 2
                  ♠ A K J 8 4
                  ♥ K 10 5 3
                  ♦ J 8 2
                  ♣ 5
```

South	West	North	East
1♠	Pass	3♦	Pass
3♠	Pass	6♠	All Pass

Opening lead: ♣4

7.

The Light Bri(d)g(e)ade

Recent historical research shows that soldiers in the 19th Century often played bridge when not engaged in battle. Today's deal comes from a game in the Crimea.

West, a British cavalryman who was sorely lacking in imagination, led the jack of diamonds against South's game. South, a French grenadier, took dummy's queen and led a heart to his king. West won the ace, muttered "Mine not to reason why," and continued obstinately with another diamond.

Spade Shift

"Can't you shift to a spade?" East pleaded after South had taken nine tricks.

West was incredulous. "Switch suits?" he protested. "You must be kidding. Besides, what if declarer had the ace and queen of spades instead of the ace of clubs and the queen of spades?"

"In that case," East responded, "he just might win the first diamond in his hand, saving an entry to dummy, and lead clubs to set up his best suit."

The next day West went out and, blindly following orders, got himself killed in an ill-fated and rather famous charge. Some people just don't profit from experience.

BIDDING QUIZ

You hold: ♠ 10 7 4 ♥ Q 9 2 ♦ Q 5 ♣ K Q J 5 3. Dealer, at your right, opens one heart. What do you say?

ANSWER: Pass. This is a sucker's overcall. You have little to gain by bidding; a two-club overcall uses up little of the opponents' bidding space, and it's hard to compete successfully in the lowest-ranking suit. You might be doubled and defeated four tricks when the opponents could make nothing.

```
Dlr: South         ♠ 10 7 4
Vul: N-S           ♥ Q 9 2
                   ♦ Q 5
                   ♣ K Q J 5 3
♠ K J 6 2                        ♠ A 9 8
♥ A 8                            ♥ J 10 6 5 4
♦ J 10 9 8 7                     ♦ 6 3
♣ 7 2                            ♣ 9 6 4
                   ♠ Q 5 3
                   ♥ K 7 3
                   ♦ A K 4 2
                   ♣ A 10 8
```

South	West	North	East
1 NT	Pass	3 NT	All Pass

Opening lead: ♦J

FRANK STEWART

8.

None of the Above

Playing some deals is like taking a multiple-choice quiz. The answer to the deal below was "None of the above."

South took the queen of spades at the first trick and saw no problem if diamonds split 3-2. When he led queen and a low diamond, however, West discarded. So much for answer (A).

South next tried (B). After taking the A-K of diamonds, he led the jack of clubs. East, though, played low, knowing dummy would never have the lead again. West won the king of clubs and continued spades.

South took his ace and tried (C); maybe his ace of clubs would drop the queen. It didn't, and down he went.

Overtakes

South can make game by trying "All of the above" — combining his chances. At the second trick, he leads the deuce of diamonds for a finesse with dummy's ten. If East wins the jack, South overtakes the queen of diamonds later and runs the diamonds for nine tricks.

If the ten of diamonds wins, South next leads the eight of clubs for a finesse. When he regains the lead, he overtakes the queen of diamonds with the king. If diamonds split 3-2, South is home; otherwise, he tries another club finesse.

BIDDING QUIZ

You hold: ♠ A Q 6 ♥ A J 3 ♦ Q 2 ♣ A 10 9 6 2. Dealer, at your right, opens one diamond. You double, and your partner responds one heart. What do you say?

ANSWER: Pass. If you double, then bid again, you promise at least 17 points. Although you have a well placed queen of spades and a five-card club suit, your queen of diamonds is probably worthless. Also, you have only three-card heart support.

```
Dir: South        ♠ 7 2
Vul: N-S          ♥ 5 4
                  ♦ A K 10 9 5 3
                  ♣ J 8 3
♠ K 9 8 4 3                      ♠ J 10 5
♥ Q 9 8 6 2                      ♥ K 10 7
♦ 4                              ♦ J 8 7 6
♣ K 5                            ♣ Q 7 4
                  ♠ A Q 6
                  ♥ A J 3
                  ♦ Q 2
                  ♣ A 10 9 6 2
```

South	West	North	East
1 NT	Pass	3 NT	All Pass

Opening lead: ♠4

9.

Dlr: South
Vul: N-S

    ♠ Q 6
    ♥ J 7 6 5
    ♦ A J 10 7 3
    ♣ 7 6

```
        N
    W       E
        S
```

    ♠ J 10 9
    ♥ K 8 3 2
    ♦ K Q 9
    ♣ Q 10 3

South	West	North	East
1 NT	Pass	2 NT	Pass
3 NT	All Pass		

West leads the ♣5, and your queen wins. Your ♣10 holds the next trick. South takes the third club with the ace and leads a diamond to dummy's ten. How do you defend?

10.

Dlr: West
Vul: N-S

    ♠ A 7 4
    ♥ 8 7
    ♦ Q 9 6 5 4
    ♣ J 5 3

    ♠ 9
    ♥ A Q 3 2
    ♦ A K J 10 3 2
    ♣ K 10

West	North	East	South
Pass	Pass	Pass	1 ♦
Pass	2 ♦	Pass	5 ♦
All Pass			

West leads the ♠Q. Plan the play.

11.

Dlr: South   ♠ Q 6
Vul: N-S   ♥ 4 2
                ♦ 9 7 2
                ♣ A K 8 7 6 3

                ♠ K 7 4
                ♥ A K Q 6 5
                ♦ A K 4
                ♣ 5 2

South	West	North	East
1♥	1♠	2♣	Pass
3 NT	All Pass		

West leads the ♠J, you put up dummy's queen, and East follows with the two. Plan the play.

12.

Dlr: South   ♠ 10 5 4
Vul: N-S   ♥ 10 7 5 3
                ♦ Q J 10 6
                ♣ A Q

```
        N                ♠ K 9 7 3
      W   E              ♥ K J 8
        S                ♦ K 5 2
                         ♣ 7 5 2
```

South	West	North	East
1 NT	Pass	2♣	Pass
2♦	Pass	3 NT	All Pass

West leads the ♥9. Plan the defense.

9.

Removing an Option

Give declarer two chances for his contract, and he'll probably get home. Give him one chance, and he may go down.

In a team match, both Souths played 3NT. They both refused the first two club leads, took the third club with the ace and then led a diamond to the ten and queen.

One East then returned the jack of spades. South took the queen and ace and tried another diamond finesse with the jack. When East won the queen, declarer had only eight tricks and knew that he needed the heart finesse for a ninth. When the king of hearts obligingly turned up onside, South made his game.

All Options

The other East saw that declarer was fated to succeed if he had time to try all his options. After winning the first diamond, this East impassively led back the eight of hearts!

South had to pick his poison. He could have finessed in hearts, but he really expected the diamonds to yield the tricks he needed. The second South therefore rose with the ace of hearts and led a diamond to finesse with the jack.

East managed to remain impassive as he won the king and cashed the king of hearts to defeat the contract.

BIDDING QUIZ

You hold: ♠ Q 6 ♥ J 7 6 5 ♦ A J 10 7 3 ♣ 7 6. Your partner opens one club, and the next player overcalls one spade. What do you say?

ANSWER: Pass (unless you play negative doubles). You aren't strong enough to bid a suit at the two level (the hearts are too weak in any case), nor can you try 1NT. The queen of spades is of doubtful worth, so unless partner can bid again, you probably won't miss anything.

```
Dlr: South          ♠ Q 6
Vul: N-S            ♥ J 7 6 5
                    ♦ A J 10 7 3
                    ♣ 7 6
      ♠ 8 7 5 2                        ♠ J 10 9
      ♥ 10 4                           ♥ K 8 3 2
      ♦ 6 5                            ♦ K Q 9
      ♣ K J 9 5 2                      ♣ Q 10 3
                    ♠ A K 4 3
                    ♥ A Q 9
                    ♦ 8 4 2
                    ♣ A 8 4
```

South	West	North	East
1 NT	Pass	2 NT	Pass
3 NT	All Pass		

Opening lead: ♣ 5

10.

Patience Rewarded

When my friend Patience (Patti, for short) heard a diamond raise, she leaped impulsively to game. No harm done; five diamonds was a good contract.

Then came the play, and Patti was still in a hurry. She took the ace of spades, drew trumps, led a club and pondered for a long time before finessing with the ten. West won the queen and led another spade. Patti ruffed, lost to the ace of clubs and later tried the heart finesse. West took the king, defeating the contract, and Patience was exhausted.

Delay Guess

Patience's plan wasn't so full of virtue. It's best to delay the crucial guess in clubs.

At the third trick, South takes the losing heart finesse. She ruffs West's spade return, cashes the ace of hearts, ruffs a heart, ruffs a spade and ruffs a heart. Only then does she lead a club.

By now, Patti knows that West had K-J-x-x of hearts, probably Q-J-10-x of spades, and one diamond. If West, a passed hand, had the ace of clubs, he surely would have doubled one diamond for takeout.

Thus, South's right play is to put up the king of clubs. When West can't produce the ace, Patience is rewarded.

BIDDING QUIZ

You hold: ♠ A 7 4 ♥ 8 7 ♦ Q 9 6 5 4 ♣ J 5 3. Your partner opens one spade, and you raise to two spades. Partner then bids three clubs. The opponents pass. What do you say?

ANSWER: Bid three spades. Partner is interested in game and says that help in clubs will be especially useful. Since you have a minimum raise with no club help at all, reject the invitation. If your queen were in clubs, you would jump to four spades.

```
Dlr: West            ♠ A 7 4
Vul: N-S             ♥ 8 7
                     ♦ Q 9 6 5 4
                     ♣ J 5 3
♠ Q J 10 3                            ♠ K 8 6 5 2
♥ K J 5 4                             ♥ 10 9 6
♦ 7                                   ♦ 8
♣ Q 9 7 4                             ♣ A 8 6 2
                     ♠ 9
                     ♥ A Q 3 2
                     ♦ A K J 10 3 2
                     ♣ K 10
```

West	North	East	South
Pass	Pass	Pass	1♦
Pass	2♦	Pass	5♦
All Pass			

Opening lead: ♠Q

11.

A Geographical Deal

This deal saw a Grecian tug-of-war.

South won the first trick with the queen of spades and led a heart from dummy. If East had played low, declarer would have done likewise, losing the trick safely to West while setting up four heart tricks (and nine in all).

East Scotched that plan by putting up the ten of hearts. South had to win, and West alertly dropped his jack.

Declarer next went to the ace of clubs and led a second heart. Once more his play got a Chile reception; East rose with the nine of hearts, again preventing South from passing the trick to West.

Not Done

South wasn't Finnished, however; he cashed a third heart. If West threw a spade, South would concede a heart to East and lose only three spades and a heart. So West threw a diamond.

Declarer then took the A-K of diamonds and king of clubs and led a club. West had to win and give South a trick with the king of spades.

"Jamaica?" North asked anxiously.

"Of course," said South. "I gave a Polished performance."

BIDDING QUIZ

You hold: ♠ A J 10 8 3 ♥ J 8 ♦ 10 6 3 ♣ Q 10 4. Your partner opens one heart, you respond one spade, and he next bids two clubs. The opponents pass. What do you say?

ANSWER: Bid two hearts, giving partner another chance if he has a strong hand. Since he surely has five hearts, the "false preference" is safe. You must not raise clubs, which promises about 11 points and four-card support, or rebid spades with only a five-card suit.

```
Dlr: South          ♠ Q 6
Vul: N-S            ♥ 4 2
                    ♦ 9 7 2
                    ♣ A K 8 7 6 3
♠ A J 10 8 3                        ♠ 9 5 2
♥ J 8                               ♥ 10 9 7 3
♦ 10 6 3                            ♦ Q J 8 5
♣ Q 10 4                            ♣ J 9
                    ♠ K 7 4
                    ♥ A K Q 6 5
                    ♦ A K 4
                    ♣ 5 2
```

South	West	North	East
1♥	1♠	2♣	Pass
3 NT	All Pass		

Opening lead: ♠J

12.

Pro Works Miracle

Aspiring players often hire professional partners for big tournaments. The pro must take straw (any aspiring player will make plenty of errors) and somehow spin it into gold.

Today's West made a typical A.P. opening lead. Though a heart lead was reasonable, the nine was too valuable a card to waste.

South played low from dummy, and the pro in the East seat put his spinning wheel in motion by following with the jack.

Spade Switch

Declarer won the queen of hearts and cashed the ace. Sure enough, East dropped the king! South then led a heart to dummy's seven, expecting to win four heart tricks, four clubs and one diamond. East took the eight of hearts and switched to spades to defeat the contract.

Most of the Wests who defended 3NT led spades, and South threw hearts as the defense took four spade tricks. Later, South took the winning diamond finesse for his contract.

The life of a bridge pro isn't easy. I don't recommend that you become one unless you're related to Rumpelstiltskin.

BIDDING QUIZ

You hold: ♠ K 9 7 3 ♥ K J 8 ♦ K 5 2 ♣ 7 5 2. Your partner opens one diamond, you respond one spade, and he raises to two spades. The opponents pass. What do you say?

ANSWER: Pass. Partner has 13 to 15 points, probably with four-card spade support. Even if he has a maximum, you are short of the values for game. Your hand has no redeeming virtues; your balanced distribution and plentiful losers are discouraging.

```
Dlr: South          ♠ 10 5 4
Vul: N-S            ♥ 10 7 5 3
                    ♦ Q J 10 6
                    ♣ A Q
♠ A J 6 2                           ♠ K 9 7 3
♥ 9 6 2                             ♥ K J 8
♦ 8 7                               ♦ K 5 2
♣ 9 8 6 4                           ♣ 7 5 2
                    ♠ Q 8
                    ♥ A Q 4
                    ♦ A 9 4 3
                    ♣ K J 10 3
```

South	West	North	East
1 NT	Pass	2♣	Pass
2♦	Pass	3 NT	All Pass

Opening lead: ♥9

13.

Dlr: South
Vul: N-S

♠ 4 3 2
♥ A 3
♦ A 9 3
♣ K 8 7 4 2

♠ A K 6 5
♥ K 9
♦ Q 10 8 5
♣ A J 5

South	West	North	East
1 NT	Pass	3 NT	All Pass

West leads the ♥7. Plan the play.

14.

Dlr: West
Vul: N-S

♠ A J 7
♥ J 7 6 4 2
♦ K J 3
♣ 10 3

♠ Q 10 6 2
♥ K Q 10 8 3
♦ 9 4
♣ A J

West	North	East	South
Pass	Pass	Pass	1♥
2♣	4♥	All Pass	

West leads the ♣6, and East plays the king. You take the ace and lead a trump. West wins the ace, cashes the ♣Q and leads a low diamond. What do you play from dummy?

15.

Dlr: West
Vul: N-S

♠ Q 7 5 2
♥ 7 5 4 3
♦ 7 2
♣ A 6 3

♠ A K 4
♥ K Q
♦ A K 5
♣ K J 9 5 4

West	North	East	South
3♦	Pass	Pass	Dbl
Pass	3♠	Pass	4 NT
Pass	5♦	Pass	6 NT
All Pass			

West leads the ♦Q. Plan the play.

16.

Dlr: North
Vul: N-S

♠ K 9 2
♥ A 7 5 3
♦ 2
♣ K J 7 4 3

♠ 10 8 6 5
♥ K Q
♦ A Q 6 4
♣ A 6 5

North	East	South	West
1♣	Dbl	Redbl	Pass
Pass	1♦	3 NT	All Pass

West leads the ♦3, and East plays the king. Plan the play.

13.

A Plan in Reserve

Look at the North-South cards in the deal below. How do you play 3NT when West leads the seven of hearts?

The instinctive play is to win the ace of hearts and try a finesse with the jack of clubs. If that was your plan, better beware of your instincts.

West wins the queen of clubs and knocks out your king of hearts. When East discards on the ace of clubs, you can take only eight tricks before the defenders get in and run the hearts.

Lead To King

You make 3NT if you have a contingency plan. Win the king of hearts at the first trick, lead a club to the king and then plan a finesse with the jack of clubs.

If the jack wins, you get at least four club tricks. If West holds only one club, you have enough entries to dummy to concede a club and return to cash the fifth club.

When East discards on the second club, you switch plans. Take the ace of clubs and lead a diamond. When West turns up with the singleton jack of diamonds, you win three diamonds and two tricks in each of the other suits to make your game.

BIDDING QUIZ

You hold: ♠ A K 6 5 ♥ K 9 ♦ Q 10 8 5 ♣ A J 5. You open 1NT (16-18), and partner responds two clubs. You bid two spades, and partner jumps to five spades. The opponents pass. What do you say?

ANSWER: Partner asks you to make a slam decision based on how many points you hold. Since you have 17, your hand lies in the middle of the 1NT range, but most of your high cards are aces and kings — a good omen for slam. Bid six spades.

```
Dlr: South          ♠ 4 3 2
Vul: N-S            ♥ A 3
                    ♦ A 9 3
                    ♣ K 8 7 4 2
♠ J 9 8                              ♠ Q 10 7
♥ Q 10 8 7 6                         ♥ J 5 4 2
♦ J                                  ♦ K 7 6 4 2
♣ Q 10 9 6                           ♣ 3
                    ♠ A K 6 5
                    ♥ K 9
                    ♦ Q 10 8 5
                    ♣ A J 5
```

South	West	North	East
1 NT	Pass	3 NT	All Pass

Opening lead: ♥7

FRANK STEWART

14.

The Name of the Blame

South committed a felony in the deal below. Kibitz the evidence and decide what it was.

Declarer won the ace of clubs at the first trick and led a trump. West won the ace, took the queen of clubs and shifted to a diamond. South promptly put up dummy's king, losing to the ace, and a squad of blue-clad police burst in and hauled him away (irritating the other players, who wanted to finish the rubber).

Can't Have Ace

At the trial, South argued that West, who had overcalled at the two level, was apt to have the ace of diamonds. Yes, said the judge, but West couldn't hold the ace of diamonds, queen of clubs, ace of hearts, and king of spades, since he hadn't opened the bidding. And if West lacked the king of spades, the contract was hopeless.

South must make a "second-degree assumption," mentally placing a key card, then following the consequences of his assumption. South should finesse with the jack of diamonds, hoping West has the king of spades and no ace of diamonds.

How to classify South's crime? I'd call it ... second-degree murder.

BIDDING QUIZ

You hold: ♠ Q 10 6 2 ♥ K Q 10 8 3 ♦ 9 4 ♣ A J. Your partner opens 1NT, and the next player passes. What do you say?

ANSWER: Bid two clubs to look for a fit in a major suit. If partner next bids two spades or two hearts, raise to game. If he bids two diamonds, denying a four-card major, jump to three hearts, promising a good hand with five hearts. Partner will raise with three-card heart support; otherwise, he will bid 3NT.

Dlr: West	♠ A J 7		
Vul: N-S	♥ J 7 6 4 2		
	♦ K J 3		
	♣ 10 3		
♠ K 8 3			♠ 9 5 4
♥ A			♥ 9 5
♦ Q 8 2			♦ A 10 7 6 5
♣ Q 8 7 6 5 2			♣ K 9 4
	♠ Q 10 6 2		
	♥ K Q 10 8 3		
	♦ 9 4		
	♣ A J		

West	North	East	South
Pass	Pass	Pass	1♥
2♣	4♥	All Pass	

Opening lead: ♣6

15.

A Hypothetical Count

Some players take an opposing preempt as a personal insult; thus, South let West's three-diamond opening goad him into a wild leap to slam.

Declarer won the first trick with the king of diamonds and led the king of hearts. East took the ace and returned the jack of hearts to South's queen. West followed suit.

South then led a club to the ace and finessed with the jack of clubs. When West discarded, the slam was doomed. Declarer salvaged 11 tricks only with complex play, ending with a heart-club squeeze against East.

Finesse

"Who would finesse with the nine of clubs?" South pleaded. "I'd look silly if I lost to the doubleton ten."

"Maybe so," North agreed, "but in that case, you could never make the slam."

To take 12 tricks, South must assume that spades will split 3-3. West has shown two hearts and probably has seven diamonds for his preempt. On the assumption that West will have three spades, he can have only one club.

So the scary finesse with the nine of clubs is indeed the correct play.

BIDDING QUIZ

You hold: ♠ 10 8 6 ♥ 8 6 ♦ Q J 10 9 8 6 3 ♣ 7. Your partner opens one club, and the next player passes. What do you say?

ANSWER: Preempt with three diamonds. If partner has a minimum hand, the opponents may be cold for game in a major. Your jump will make it hard for them to get there. If partner has a fair hand, you will make your bid, and if he has a good hand, he may raise you to game or try 3NT.

```
Dlr: West          ♠ Q 7 5 2
Vul: N-S           ♥ 7 5 4 3
                   ♦ 7 2
                   ♣ A 6 3
♠ 10 8 6                            ♠ J 9 3
♥ 8 6                               ♥ A J 10 9 2
♦ Q J 10 9 8 6 3                    ♦ 4
♣ 7                                 ♣ Q 10 8 2
                   ♠ A K 4
                   ♥ K Q
                   ♦ A K 5
                   ♣ K J 9 5 4
```

West	North	East	South
3♦	Pass	Pass	Dbl
Pass	3♠	Pass	4 NT
Pass	5♦	Pass	6 NT
All Pass			

Opening lead: ♦ Q

16.

Erdos's Safety Play

Ivan Erdos, one of bridge's first professional players, died in 1967 at the age of 43. Erdos, born in Budapest, was known as a fine bidding tactician, but he was also a capable declarer.

To try matching Erdos's play in the deal below, cover the East-West cards. East plays the king of diamonds at the first trick.

Erdos took the ace of diamonds and led a low club. When West contributed the eight, Ivan played LOW from dummy.

Erdos won the next diamond with the queen, took the K-Q of hearts and ace of clubs, and finessed with the jack of clubs. Two more clubs and the ace of hearts gave him nine tricks.

Cashes Ace

Many declarers failed in 3NT when they cashed the ace of clubs at the second trick and then finessed with the jack of clubs. This approach ignored the clear danger that East would be short in clubs for his take-out double.

When East discarded on the second club, entries were so tangled that nine tricks were impossible.

Erdos's play virtually assured the contract.

BIDDING QUIZ

You hold: ♠ 10 8 6 5 ♥ K Q ♦ A Q 6 4 ♣ A 6 5. You open one diamond, and your partner responds one heart. You bid one spade, he returns to two diamonds. The opponents pass. What do you say?

ANSWER: Game is unlikely, since partner's preference promises at most nine points. Although he could have a magic hand with A-J-x-x-x of hearts and the king of diamonds, it doesn't pay to credit him with specific cards. Pass.

```
Dlr: North            ♠ K 9 2
Vul: N-S              ♥ A 7 5 3
                      ♦ 2
                      ♣ K J 7 4 3
♠ 7 4                                  ♠ A Q J 3
♥ 10 8 4 2                             ♥ J 9 6
♦ 9 7 3                                ♦ K J 10 8 5
♣ Q 10 9 8                             ♣ 2
                      ♠ 10 8 6 5
                      ♥ K Q
                      ♦ A Q 6 4
                      ♣ A 6 5
```

North	East	South	West
1♣	Dbl	Redbl	Pass
Pass	1♦	3 NT	All Pass

Opening lead: ♦3

17.

Dlr: North   ♠ 9 4
Vul: N-S   ♥ A 9 3
             ♦ A 10 5
             ♣ K Q J 7 3

             ♠ Q 7 5 2
             ♥ K Q 4
             ♦ K J 3
             ♣ 8 4 2

North	East	South	West
1♣	1♠	2 NT	Pass
3 NT	All Pass		

West leads the ♠8. Plan the play.

18.

Dlr: North   ♠ A 5
Vul: N-S   ♥ Q J 10 7 5 4 2
             ♦ A
             ♣ J 7 4

♠ J 9 3
♥ A K
♦ 10 9 7 6 5 4 2
♣ 9

```
      N
  W       E
      S
```

North	East	South	West
1♥	2♣	2♠	Pass
3♥	Pass	3♠	Pass
4♠	All Pass		

You lead the ♣9, and East wins the queen. Plan the defense.

19.

Dlr: South
Vul: N-S

    ♠ A Q 3
    ♥ K J 8 5 2
    ♦ K 5 4 2
    ♣ Q

    ♠ 10 7 4
    ♥ A 10 9
    ♦ A Q 3
    ♣ A 10 4 2

South	West	North	East
1♣	Pass	1♥	Pass
1 NT	Pass	3 NT	All Pass

West leads the ♠6. Plan the play.

20.

Dlr: South
Vul: N-S

    ♠ 8 4 2
    ♥ 7 2
    ♦ J 9 7 5 4 2
    ♣ Q 3

    ♠ A K
    ♥ K Q J 3
    ♦ A K Q
    ♣ A J 5 2

South	West	North	East
3 NT	Pass	Pass	Pass

West leads the ♠5; East plays the queen. Plan the play.

17.

A Spicy Deal

South in the deal below was partnering his wife Margaret in a kitchen bridge game. At 3NT, East put in the ten of spades at the first trick, and South grabbed the queen.

Declarer next led a club. Cumin in with the ace, West (her name was Rosemary) led her last spade, and East (her's was Ginger) ran off four spade tricks to beat the game. This result got a chili response from Margaret, who peppered her spouse with sage advice on dummy play and then salted his wounds by saying he couldn't cut the mustard.

Crazy

Declarer told his partner she was crazy (his exact words were "You're a nut, Meg"), whereupon she nearly clove his head with a carving knife. Aghast, South conceded that his wife might be parsley correct. "I mint to let the ten of spades win at the first trick," he pleaded, and tried to curry favor by suggesting a new dill.

North has my sympathy. Yes, if South bides his thyme and refuses the first trick, the defense can win only three spade tricks and a club.

By now, I suppose, you can guess that South's name was Herb. What else?

BIDDING QUIZ

You hold: ♠ A K J 10 3 ♥ 10 6 2 ♦ Q 9 2 ♣ 6 5. Your partner opens 1NT, and the next player passes. What do you say?

ANSWER: Bid three spades. This bid is forcing and asks your partner to raise with three or four cards in spades or return to 3NT with two. Don't err by bidding only two spades. Partner will pass, expecting you to have a long suit but no interest in game.

```
Dlr: North        ♠ 9 4
Vul: N-S          ♥ A 9 3
                  ♦ A 10 5
                  ♣ K Q J 7 3
  ♠ 8 6                          ♠ A K J 10 3
  ♥ J 8 7 5                      ♥ 10 6 2
  ♦ 8 7 6 4                      ♦ Q 9 2
  ♣ A 10 9                       ♣ 6 5
                  ♠ Q 7 5 2
                  ♥ K Q 4
                  ♦ K J 3
                  ♣ 8 4 2
```

North	East	South	West
1♣	1♠	2 NT	Pass
3 NT	All Pass		

Opening lead: ♠8

18.

The Wurst Defense?

West, a shameless ham, saw a chance for a flamboyant discard in the deal below.

When South followed with the five and eight of clubs under East's queen and king, West knew that declarer still had the ten of clubs left; therefore, East's ace of clubs would be a "wiener."

With two discards coming, West threw a diamond at the second trick, a play only a turkey would make; and when East next led the ace of clubs, West matched it with the ace of hearts!

One-trick Set

East next led a heart. West had his king on the table, ready to score up a one-trick set, but South unexpectedly ruffed (the unkindest coldcut of all). South then drew trumps and claimed.

"I never sausage discards," East observed. "What baloney!"

With West more interested in theatrics than tight defense, East was lucky South had been in a mere game and not a grand salami. At the second and third tricks, West must discard the A-K of hearts. When East then leads a heart, West's J-9-3 of trumps bring home the bacon (the setting trick) no matter whether South ruffs high or low.

BIDDING QUIZ

You hold: ♠ K Q 10 8 6 2 ♥ None ♦ K Q J 3 ♣ 10 8 5. Your partner opens 1NT, and you respond three spades. Partner raises to four spades. The opponents pass. What do you say?

ANSWER: Slam may be cold if partner has the right cards, but the five level may be too high if he is weak in clubs. Also, no good bid is available to try for slam. (To make your first cuebid in a void suit is too likely to mislead partner.) Pass and take the probable game.

```
Dlr: North          ♠ A 5
Vul: N-S            ♥ Q J 10 7 5 4 2
                    ♦ A
                    ♣ J 7 4
♠ J 9 3                              ♠ 7 4
♥ A K                                ♥ 9 8 6 3
♦ 10 9 7 6 5 4 2                     ♦ 8
♣ 9                                  ♣ A K Q 6 3 2
                    ♠ K Q 10 8 6 2
                    ♥ None
                    ♦ K Q J 3
                    ♣ 10 8 5
```

North	East	South	West
1♥	2♣	2♠	Pass
3♥	Pass	3♠	Pass
4♠	All Pass		

Opening lead: ♣9

19.

Dubious Record

I don't know the record for finesses lost in one deal, but South in the deal below may own it.

South's streak began when he played a low spade from dummy at the first trick. East's jack won, and South was 0-for-1 in the finesse department.

East returned a club, and declarer had to refuse the trick. (If declarer won and then misguessed the queen of hearts, the defenders might get three clubs, a heart and a spade.) West took the king of clubs (0-for-2) and led a second spade. Dummy's queen lost to the king (0-for-3), and East led another club.

Cashes Club

West took South's ten with the jack (0-for-4) and returned a club to the ace. When South next led a heart to the jack, East produced the queen (0-for-5) and cashed a club. Down two.

South's very first finesse was his downfall. He assures his contract if he takes the ace of spades and plans a finesse with the jack of hearts. If East wins the queen, he can't lead a spade profitably. When South regains the lead, he will have at least nine tricks to cash.

BIDDING QUIZ

You hold: ♠ 10 7 4 ♥ A 10 9 ♦ A Q 3 ♣ A 10 4 2. Your partner opens one spade, and you respond 2NT. He next bids three hearts. The opponents pass. What do you say?

ANSWER: Partner is worried about notrump, and you should be concerned also; your aces in the minor suits suggest playing at a suit contract. Bid three spades to show your support for partner's first suit and see how he reacts.

	♠ A Q 3	
Dlr: South	♥ K J 8 5 2	
Vul: N-S	♦ K 5 4 2	
	♣ Q	

♠ 6 5 2		♠ K J 9 8
♥ 7 6		♥ Q 4 3
♦ J 9 8 7		♦ 10 6
♣ K J 9 5		♣ 8 7 6 3

	♠ 10 7 4	
	♥ A 10 9	
	♦ A Q 3	
	♣ A 10 4 2	

South	West	North	East
1♣	Pass	1♥	Pass
1 NT	Pass	3 NT	All Pass

Opening lead: ♠6

20.

Gaining Time

Beginners are taught to lead toward their high cards. It's good advice, but not always the best.

South won the first trick, unblocked the A-K-Q of diamonds and led a club to the queen, trying to reach the diamond tricks that lay tantalizingly in dummy. East took the king of clubs and returned a spade. When West won the ace of hearts, he cashed his spades to defeat the contract.

"We can make a slam in diamonds," South told his partner, "but at notrump I can't use your long suit. Maybe you should've bid diamonds."

Out Of Reach

South was right that North's diamonds were out of reach, but wrong that North should bid (although if North had suspected that South would mangle 3NT, he definitely would have been willing to try his luck at the diamond slam).

After South cashes the high diamonds, he should lead the jack of clubs. East must refuse the trick, else South will use the queen of clubs to reach dummy's diamonds. South can then lead the king of hearts to force the ace, and he has two spades, two clubs, three diamonds and two hearts for his game.

BIDDING QUIZ

You hold: ♠ 8 4 2 ♥ 7 2 ♦ J 9 7 5 4 2 ♣ Q 3. Your partner deals and opens 1NT, and the next player passes. What do you say?

ANSWER: If you trust your partner, bid two diamonds, a weak response that asks him to pass. If partner is untrustworthy, pass to avoid disaster. A bad partner may jump to 3NT or commit some other indiscretion over two diamonds, and the opponents may smell blood and double.

Dlr: South	♠ 8 4 2		
Vul: N-S	♥ 7 2		
	♦ J 9 7 5 4 2		
	♣ Q 3		

♠ J 10 6 5 3		♠ Q 9 7
♥ A 9 4		♥ 10 8 6 5
♦ 10		♦ 8 6 3
♣ 10 8 6 4		♣ K 9 7

♠ A K
♥ K Q J 3
♦ A K Q
♣ A J 5 2

South	West	North	East
3 NT	Pass	Pass	Pass

Opening lead: ♠ 5

21.

Dlr: South		♠ K 5	
Vul: N-S		♥ 2	
		♦ A Q J 3 2	
		♣ 10 7 6 5 4	

♠ A 7 4 2
♥ A K 10
♦ 10 6 5
♣ K Q 3

South	West	North	East
1 NT	Pass	3♦	Pass
3 NT	All Pass		

West leads the ♥6, and East plays the jack. Plan the play.

22.

♠ 9 6 3
♥ K 7 3
♦ 10 5 3
♣ K 10 4 2

North	East	South	West
1♥	2♦	2♠	Pass
3♠	Pass	3 NT	Pass
4♠	All Pass		

What should West lead?

23.

Dlr: East   ♠ 10 5
Vul: N-S   ♥ A Q J 3
                     ♦ 10 7 5 4
                     ♣ Q 7 3

                     ♠ K 6 2
                     ♥ K 5 2
                     ♦ K Q J 9
                     ♣ K J 8

East	South	West	North
1♦	1 NT	Pass	3 NT
All Pass			

West leads the ♣4, and East contributes the queen. How do you play?

24.

Dlr: North   ♠ J 10 3
Vul: N-S   ♥ J 10 4
                     ♦ A J 8 5 2
                     ♣ A K

                     ♠ K 5
                     ♥ A Q 9 8 5 2
                     ♦ K 7 3
                     ♣ 7 4

North	East	South	West
1♦	Pass	1♥	Pass
1 NT	Pass	4♥	All Pass

West leads the ♣Q. Plan the play.

21.

Tough Test

You can be proud if you make this 3NT contract. East puts up the jack of hearts at the first trick. How do you play?

If you win and try a diamond finesse, you're in for trouble. East takes the king and returns a heart, setting up West's suit. Since you have only eight tricks, you must lead a club, and West wins the ace and cashes his hearts.

At the second trick, you must instead lead a diamond to the ace and continue with a club from dummy. A losing diamond finesse will give East the lead too soon, but you don't mind losing an early club trick to West.

Many Chances

If your king of clubs wins, shift to diamonds, setting up four diamond tricks, a club, two hearts and two spades. If East were to rise with the ace of clubs to return a heart, you would still be a favorite to make the contract.

As the cards lie, West takes the king of clubs with his ace, but he can do nothing to hurt you.

It isn't safe to cross to the king of spades at Trick Two for a club lead. If West continued spades when he won the ace of clubs, you might lose three spades, a club and a diamond.

BIDDING QUIZ

You hold: ♠ Q J 10 8 6 ♥ J 9 5 ♦ K 9 ♣ J 9 8. Your partner opens one diamond, you bid one spade, and he next jumps to three clubs. The opponents pass. What do you say?

ANSWER: Since partner's jump shift is forcing to game, you can afford to mark time with a rebid of three spades. You will pass if partner next raises to four spades or bids 3NT. If he bids four clubs or four diamonds, raise to game in the minor suit.

```
Dlr: South        ♠ K 5
Vul: N-S          ♥ 2
                  ♦ A Q J 3 2
                  ♣ 10 7 6 5 4
♠ 9 3                              ♠ Q J 10 8 6
♥ Q 8 7 6 4 3                      ♥ J 9 5
♦ 8 7 4                            ♦ K 9
♣ A 2                              ♣ J 9 8
                  ♠ A 7 4 2
                  ♥ A K 10
                  ♦ 10 6 5
                  ♣ K Q 3
```

South	West	North	East
1 NT	Pass	3♦	Pass
3 NT	All Pass		

Opening lead: ♥6

22.

Your Suit or Partner's?

Being the opening leader takes courage. If you lead partner's suit when a different lead would work better, he'll grumble a bit; but if you don't lead his suit and you're wrong, he'll roast you.

West in the deal below didn't want to be roasted; he led a diamond against four spades. East won and shifted, too late, to a club.

South took the ace of clubs, came to the ace of trumps and threw a club on the king of diamonds. He next led a heart, and the defenders could get only one heart and one club.

Innocent Victim

West claimed he was an innocent victim, but risking a visit to the roasting pit was correct this time.

North, who insisted on a suit contract, must be short in diamonds. South, who bid notrump, surely has diamond strength. It shouldn't be too hard, therefore, for West to visualize the possible course of the play.

Since East-West will surely need a club trick or two, West should lead a club. A diamond lead can wait; the ace, if East holds it, will probably be the only diamond trick for the defense.

BIDDING QUIZ

You hold: ♠ A Q J 8 4 ♥ 9 6 ♦ K J 8 ♣ J 7 6. You open one spade, and your partner responds two hearts. You rebid two spades, he rebids three hearts. The opponents pass. What do you say?

ANSWER: Partner promises six or seven hearts with a minimum two-over-one response. With a better hand, he would jump to four hearts or bid a new suit to force you. Since you are allowed to hit the brakes on this auction with a minimum opening bid, pass.

Dlr: North	♠ K 10 7 2		
Vul: N-S	♥ A J 10 5 4		
	♦ 7		
	♣ A 8 5		
♠ 9 6 3		♠ 5	
♥ K 7 3		♥ Q 8 2	
♦ 10 5 3		♦ A Q 9 6 4 2	
♣ K 10 4 2		♣ Q 9 3	
	♠ A Q J 8 4		
	♥ 9 6		
	♦ K J 8		
	♣ J 7 6		

North	East	South	West
1♥	2♦	2♠	Pass
3♠	Pass	3 NT	Pass
4♠	All Pass		

Opening lead: ??

23.

Fish Story

This deal features a whale of a defensive play by East and a sucker play by declarer.

Hoping his partner would forgive him for not leading a diamond, West started with a spade. When dummy played low, East — a bridge-table barracuda — put in the queen. South took the bait and won his king of spades (just for the halibut, I suppose).

South next led a diamond. East took the ace and reeled declarer in by leading the ace and a low spade. West cashed his spades, and the ace of clubs completed a two-trick set.

Has Aces

South floundered badly when he took the king of spades. Since East, who opened the bidding, surely has the missing aces, South knows that something is fishy. He must refuse the first trick, after which West can't get the long spades. Declarer loses only two spades, a club and a diamond.

"Holy mackerel," sighed North, having lost a rubber to the tuna $50. "Not to carp, but three notrump was cold."

And all South could say in reply was, "Shut up and deal the cods."

BIDDING QUIZ

You hold: ♠ A Q 8 ♥ 8 4 ♦ A 8 6 3 2 ♣ A 10 2. You open one diamond, and partner responds one heart. You bid 1NT, he jumps to three hearts. The opponents pass. What do you say?

ANSWER: Even if you play partner's jump as not forcing, bid 3NT. Your hand is maximum for a 1NT rebid, and your high cards are mostly aces. Since your bidding promised at least a doubleton heart, partner can still return to hearts with a distributional hand.

```
Dlr: East          ♠ 10 5
Vul: N-S           ♥ A Q J 3
                   ♦ 10 7 5 4
                   ♣ Q 7 3
  ♠ J 9 7 4 3                      ♠ A Q 8
  ♥ 10 9 7 6                       ♥ 8 4
  ♦ None                           ♦ A 8 6 3 2
  ♣ 9 6 5 4                        ♣ A 10 2
                   ♠ K 6 2
                   ♥ K 5 2
                   ♦ K Q J 9
                   ♣ K J 8
```

East	South	West	North
1♦	1 NT	Pass	3 NT
All Pass			

Opening lead: ♠4

24.

Pessimism Pays

In a match between a team of wide-eyed optimists and a team of confirmed pessimists, I'd bet on the gloom-and-doomers every time.

In the deal below, the optimist takes the ace of clubs, loses a trump finesse, wins the next club and draws trumps. He then cashes the king of diamonds and blithely finesses with the jack of diamonds.

If West held Q-x-x of diamonds, South's optimism would produce 12 tricks. As the cards lie, East wins the queen and leads a spade, and West takes the queen and ace. South is down one, but being an optimist, he'll try the same approach next time.

Tenth Trick

The play starts the same way at the other table, but the pessimistic South expects the queen of diamonds and both high spades to be wrong. He therefore leads the king of spades after drawing trumps. When South regains the lead, he knocks out the queen of spades, setting up dummy's jack for the tenth trick.

Optimism is a noble trait, even at bridge; still, players do best who realize that finesses sometimes lose.

BIDDING QUIZ

You hold: ♠ 8 7 6 4 ♥ 7 3 ♦ Q 10 9 ♣ 9 8 6 2. Your partner opens two spades (strong), and you bid 2NT. Partner rebids three spades. The opponents pass. What do you say?

ANSWER: Bid four spades. Many pairs agree that you may pass here if you have no sign of a trick. While your hand is nothing to shout about, you hold four trumps, a ruffing value in hearts and a possible diamond trick. To pass when a game is at stake would be cowardly.

```
Dlr: North          ♠ J 10 3
Vul: N-S            ♥ J 10 4
                    ♦ A J 8 5 2
                    ♣ A K
  ♠ A Q 9 2                          ♠ 8 7 6 4
  ♥ K 6                              ♥ 7 3
  ♦ 6 4                              ♦ Q 10 9
  ♣ Q J 10 5 3                       ♣ 9 8 6 2
                    ♠ K 5
                    ♥ A Q 9 8 5 2
                    ♦ K 7 3
                    ♣ 7 4
```

North	East	South	West
1♦	Pass	1♥	Pass
1 NT	Pass	4♥	All Pass

Opening lead: ♣Q

25.

Dlr: South
Vul: N-S

♠ 8 3
♥ Q 5 4 2
♦ Q 3
♣ K Q 10 5 2

```
        N
    W       E
        S
```

♠ A Q 5
♥ 10 9 8 3
♦ 9 7 5
♣ 9 8 4

South	West	North	East
1 NT	Pass	2♣	Pass
2♦	Pass	3 NT	All Pass

West leads the ♠4. Plan the defense.

26.

Dlr: West
Vul: N-S

♠ K 10
♥ Q 10 6
♦ A K Q 10 5
♣ 7 4 3

♠ J 9 7 4
♥ A 5 2
♦ J 3
♣ A K 8 5

```
        N
    W       E
        S
```

West	North	East	South
1♣	1♦	Pass	1♥
Pass	2♥	Pass	4♥
All Pass			

You lead the ♣K, East plays the deuce, and declarer follows with the six. How do you continue?

27.

Dlr: North
Vul: N-S

        ♠ 5
        ♥ K J 7
        ♦ A Q 5 4 2
        ♣ A Q 6 2

        ♠ A J 4 3 2
        ♥ Q 10 9 8 6
        ♦ 3
        ♣ 7 4

North	East	South	West
1♦	Pass	1♠	Pass
2♣	Pass	2♥	Pass
3♥	Pass	4♥	All Pass

West leads a trump, alas. East wins the ace and returns a trump. West follows. Plan the play.

28.

Dlr: East
Vul: Both

        ♠ J 10 3
        ♥ K 7 5 3
        ♦ A 8 2
        ♣ 10 7 3

        ♠ A Q 9 7 5
        ♥ J 10 9
        ♦ 3
        ♣ A K J 4

East	South	West	South
1♥	1♠	Pass	2♠
Pass	4♠	All Pass	

West leads the ♥2. Plan the play.

25.

A Little Learning

East knew that a defender in third seat could profitably play the queen from A-Q-x as a way to preserve communications. When West led a low spade against South's 3NT, East was therefore ready with the queen of spades.

East's play did what it was supposed to do; South had to go ahead and take his king of spades. (For all South knew, West had led from A-J-x-x-x, and then to hold off would cause an embarrassing disaster.)

Set To Play Ace

South next led the jack of hearts from his hand, and West won the ace. East was all set to play his ace of spades at the next trick and return a spade, but something unforeseen happened: poor West naturally placed South with the A-K of spades! Thinking that his only chance was to find East with the ace of diamonds, West shifted to a diamond, and South made his game.

A little learning at bridge is a dangerous thing. Beware of the learned third-hand play of the queen from A-Q-x when your partner will probably regain the lead before you do!

BIDDING QUIZ

You hold: ♠ A Q 5 ♥ 10 9 8 3 ♦ 9 7 5 ♣ 9 8 4. Your partner opens one diamond, you respond one heart, and he jumps to three diamonds. The opponents pass. What do you say?

ANSWER: Pass. Partner's jump promises 15 to 18 high-card points and six or seven good diamonds. A jump in a new suit would force you to keep bidding. This jump is invitational, however, and you have nothing left over from your first response.

```
Dlr: South        ♠ 8 3
Vul: N-S          ♥ Q 5 4 2
                  ♦ Q 3
                  ♣ K Q 10 5 2
   ♠ J 9 7 4 2                    ♠ A Q 5
   ♥ A 6                          ♥ 10 9 8 3
   ♦ K J 10 4                     ♦ 9 7 5
   ♣ 7 6                          ♣ 9 8 4
                  ♠ K 10 6
                  ♥ K J 7
                  ♦ A 8 6 2
                  ♣ A J 3
```

South	West	North	East
1 NT	Pass	2♣	Pass
2♦	Pass	3 NT	All Pass

Opening lead: ♠4

26.

Red, Green, Yellow

Bridge signals and traffic signals are not quite alike. Although a high card says "go," a low card can mean either "stop" or "caution."

When West saw East play the deuce of clubs at the first trick, he shifted to a spade. South swiftly took three high spades to throw a club from dummy and then led a trump.

West won his ace immediately, cashed the ace of clubs and led a third club, but South ruffed high in dummy, drew trumps and claimed his game.

Demands Shift?

West treated partner's deuce of clubs as a red light, asking for a shift. Since the play of a low card may be only noncommittal, though, West should continue with the ace of clubs at Trick Two. (Note that East can't signal with the queen of clubs, which would promise the jack or a singleton queen.) Since dummy's diamonds will provide discards, another club lead can lose nothing even if South has Q-x-x. Also, even if the defense has a spade trick to take, a spade shift can wait.

This time, only a club continuation beats the contract. East ruffs the third club, and West's high trump takes the setting trick.

BIDDING QUIZ

You hold: ♠ J 9 7 4 ♥ A 5 2 ♦ J 3 ♣ A K 8 5. Dealer, at your right, opens one diamond, and you double. Your partner bids two spades. The opponents pass. What do you say?

ANSWER: Pass. Partner's jump is invitational, not forcing, and promises about 10 points. With fewer points (even with no points at all), he would usually bid his best suit as cheaply as possible. Since you have nothing extra for your takeout double, let him out at a partscore.

```
Dlr: West          ♠ K 10
Vul: N-S           ♥ Q 10 6
                   ♦ A K Q 10 5
                   ♣ 7 4 3
♠ J 9 7 4                         ♠ 8 6 5 2
♥ A 5 2                           ♥ 7 3
♦ J 3                             ♦ 9 8 7 4 2
♣ A K 8 5                         ♣ Q 2
                   ♠ A Q 3
                   ♥ K J 9 8 4
                   ♦ 6
                   ♣ J 10 9 6
```

West	North	East	South
1♣	1♦	Pass	1♥
Pass	2♥	Pass	4♥
All Pass			

Opening lead: ♣K

27.

Hard Work Rewarded

South in this deal has an easy time if West leads the ♣J. South grabs the ace of clubs and embarks on a crossruff: ace of spades, spade ruff, ace of diamonds, diamond ruff, spade ruff, diamond ruff, spade ruff with dummy's last trump.

Whether or not East overruffs with the ace, ten tricks are there, and declarer has barely worked up a sweat.

South sweats profusely if West leads a trump. East wins and returns a trump. Since South can then ruff only one spade in dummy, he must try to set up diamonds.

Spade Ruff

At the third trick, South risks a finesse with the queen of diamonds. (South doesn't try the club finesse because he needs a diamond finesse in any case.) He then cashes the ace of diamonds, ruffs a diamond, takes the ace of spades, ruffs a spade and ruffs another diamond. After drawing trumps, South crosses to the ace of clubs and, breathing hard, cashes the good diamond to make his game.

It's a shame that a declarer who must work that hard scores no extra points.

BIDDING QUIZ

You hold: ♠ K 10 8 7 ♥ 5 2 ♦ K 10 8 6 ♣ J 10 3. Dealer, at your left, opens one heart, and your partner overcalls two clubs. The next player raises to two hearts. What do you say?

ANSWER: Bid three clubs. Partner promises a good suit and at least a fair hand. Since you have club support and two kings, you must compete. A modern expert might suggest length in the unbid suits with a "responsive double," but you can't spring strange conventions on your partner without prior discussion.

```
Dlr: North        ♠ 5
Vul: N-S          ♥ K J 7
                  ♦ A Q 5 4 2
                  ♣ A Q 6 2
♠ K 10 8 7                      ♠ Q 9 6
♥ 5 2                           ♥ A 4 3
♦ K 10 8 6                      ♦ J 9 7
♣ J 10 3                        ♣ K 9 8 5
                  ♠ A J 4 3 2
                  ♥ Q 10 9 8 6
                  ♦ 3
                  ♣ 7 4
```

North	East	South	West
1♦	Pass	1♠	Pass
2♣	Pass	2♥	Pass
3♥	Pass	4♥	All Pass

Opening lead: ♥2

28.

Deception Saves Bacon

Once upon a time there were three little pigs, each playing the deal below at four spades in a duplicate event. At each table, East, a Big Bad Wolf, took the first trick with the queen of hearts. (All the East players in this game were unsavory characters.)

The first little pig falsecarded with his jack of hearts, but the Wolf knew that West wouldn't lead the deuce of hearts from 10-9-2. The B.B.W. took the ace of hearts and gave West a ruff. The queen of clubs defeated the contract, and after the game, the Wolf ate up the little pig out of sheer disrespect for his dummy play.

Pig #2 followed with the nine of hearts at the first trick, but East knew that West wouldn't lead low from J-10-2. Again South was defeated — and eaten.

Club Shift

The third little pig survived by playing the ten of hearts at Trick One. Now East wasn't sure what to do; West *would* lead the deuce from J-9-2. Finally, this Wolf shifted to clubs, and South made his game.

Our fairy tale has a happy ending. The Big Bad Wolf was so impressed by declarer's good play that he not only declined to eat him, he made a date to play with him in the next week's duplicate.

BIDDING QUIZ

You hold: ♠ K 4 ♥ A Q 8 6 4 ♦ K J 7 5 ♣ 9 2. Your partner opens one club, you bid one heart, and he jumps to four hearts. The opponents pass. What do you say?

ANSWER: Bid six hearts (or 4NT, if you want to go through the motions of Blackwood). Partner's jump to game is not a signoff; it promises 19 or 20 points and suggests balanced distribution. Since the values for a small slam are there, don't get cold feet. Bid it!

Dlr: East	♠ J 10 3		
Vul: Both	♥ K 7 5 3		
	♦ A 8 2		
	♣ 10 7 3		

♠ 8 6 2		♠ K 4
♥ 2		♥ A Q 8 6 4
♦ Q 10 9 6 4		♦ K J 7 5
♣ Q 8 6 5		♣ 9 2

	♠ A Q 9 7 5
	♥ J 10 9
	♦ 3
	♣ A K J 4

East	South	West	South
1♥	1♠	Pass	2♠
Pass	4♠	All Pass	

Opening lead: ♥2

29

Dlr: South
Vul: N-S

♠ 7 5 2
♥ A 6 4
♦ A Q J 10 9
♣ A K

```
        N
    W       E
        S
```

♠ K 10 8
♥ 9 3
♦ K 7 5 3
♣ J 9 7 4

South	West	North	East
Pass	Pass	1♦	Pass
1 NT	Pass	3 NT	All Pass

West leads the ♥Q. Declarer wins dummy's ace, cashes the
♣AK and leads the ♦Q. How do you defend? (Plan well ahead.)

30.

Dlr: South
Vul: N-S

♠ A 6 5
♥ 5 3
♦ A Q 7
♣ 10 8 7 5 4

```
        N
    W       E
        S
```

♠ J 3
♥ K 9 4
♦ K 6 5 4
♣ Q J 9 2

South	West	North	East
1♦	Pass	2♣	Pass
3 NT	All Pass		

West leads the ♥2, and your king loses to South's ace. Next,
South leads the ♦3: nine, queen. How do you defend?

31.

Dlr: South
Vul: N-S

♠ 9 7
♥ J 4
♦ Q J 5 3
♣ A Q 10 7 3

♠ K Q 2
♥ A 7 5
♦ A K 2
♣ J 9 4 2

South	West	North	East
1 NT	Pass	3 NT	All Pass

West leads the ♠3. Plan the play.

32.

Dlr: North
Vul: N-S

♠ K 7
♥ K 10 8
♦ A Q J 4
♣ K 7 5 3

♠ A 9 2
♥ A J 5 3 2
♦ 5 3 2
♣ A 8

North	East	South	West
1 NT	Pass	3♥	Pass
4♥	Pass	5♥	Pass
6♥	All Pass		

West leads the ♥4. Plan the play.

29.

Blue and Gray

After the terms of surrender had been signed in the McLean house near Appomattox Courthouse, the tired leaders of the Union and Confederate armies wanted to unwind. General Lee proposed a bridge game; he, of course, sat South.

Lee won the heart opening lead in dummy (if he refuses the first trick, a spade shift will set him). After thoughtfully stroking his beard, he unblocked the A-K of clubs and led the queen of diamonds.

General Grant, East, played low. He played low again when Lee continued with the jack of diamonds.

Spade Entry

Since Lee could then get only three diamond tricks, he next led a spade. Grant rose with the king and led his last heart. The ace of spades remained as an entry to West's established hearts, and Lee had to surrender (again).

Grant's play of the king of spades couldn't cost; if Lee held the ace, he had three diamond tricks, two hearts, three clubs and a spade.

To put up the king of spades was also necessary to beat the game. Grant, an able strategist, knew it was vital to set up the defenders' long suit while preserving West's entry.

BIDDING QUIZ

You hold: ♠ K 10 8 ♥ 9 3 ♦ K 7 5 3 ♣ J 9 7 4. Your partner opens two spades (strong), and you raise to three spades. He next bids four diamonds. The opponents pass. What do you say?

ANSWER: Since you have agreed on a trump suit, partner's second bid doesn't guarantee length. Instead, he indicates slam interest with a diamond "control" (surely the ace). Bid five diamonds, promising the king of diamonds. If partner goes on to six diamonds, you may pass.

```
Dlr: South        ♠ 7 5 2
Vul: N-S          ♥ A 6 4
                  ♦ A Q J 10 9
                  ♣ A K
♠ A 9 6 4                      ♠ K 10 8
♥ Q J 10 8 5                   ♥ 9 3
♦ 8                            ♦ K 7 5 3
♣ 8 6 3                        ♣ J 9 7 4
                  ♠ Q J 3
                  ♥ K 7 2
                  ♦ 6 4 2
                  ♣ Q 10 5 2
```

South	West	North	East
Pass	Pass	1♦	Pass
1 NT	Pass	3 NT	All Pass

Opening lead: ♥Q

30.

"Bad" Bid Works Well

Though your own auctions are undoubtedly flawless, you'll meet other players who have their own quaint ideas about bidding. Don't let such players bamboozle you.

South took the ace of hearts at the first trick, capturing East's king, and led a diamond to the nine, queen and king. After East returned a heart, declarer could have made an overtrick with a squeeze-endplay against West; instead, he settled for nine easy tricks.

"Don't you need balanced distribution for that jump to three notrump?" East demanded upon seeing South's bare king of clubs; but South too was busy adding up the score to reply.

Strange Bidding

Despite the strange bidding, East had clues to the winning defense. West's lead of the deuce of hearts indicated a four-card suit, so South also held four hearts; West would prefer to lead from a five-card spade suit if he had one, so South had four spades; West signalled with the nine of diamonds, suggesting one or two diamonds, so South had at least four diamonds.

Since declarer could have at most one club, East should have switched to the deuce of clubs at the third trick.

BIDDING QUIZ

You hold: ♠ K Q 9 7 ♥ A Q J 6 ♦ J 10 8 3 ♣ K. Dealer, at your right, opens one club. You double, and your partner responds one spade. The opponents pass. What do you say?

ANSWER: Raise to two spades, but just barely. You need about 17 points to bid again if partner responds cheaply to your takeout double. (Remember, he may be broke.) Since your king of clubs is probably worthless, you'll reject if partner tries for game.

```
Dlr: South          ♠ A 6 5
Vul: N-S            ♥ 5 3
                    ♦ A Q 7
                    ♣ 10 8 7 5 4

♠ 10 8 4 2                        ♠ J 3
♥ 10 8 7 2                        ♥ K 9 4
♦ 9 2                             ♦ K 6 5 4
♣ A 6 3                           ♣ Q J 9 2

                    ♠ K Q 9 7
                    ♥ A Q J 6
                    ♦ J 10 8 3
                    ♣ K
```

South	West	North	East
1♦	Pass	2♣	Pass
3 NT	All Pass		

Opening lead: ♥2

31.

Haste Makes Contract

I usually report the downfall of those who play in haste to the first trick. Not so in this deal.

South expected to win the opening lead; he assumed that West had led from a strong spade suit. Unfortunately (or so it seemed at the time), South's haste betrayed him. He tossed out his queen of spades at the first trick, heedless of East's unexpected play of the ace.

Struggling to keep his composure, South won the spade return and lost a club finesse. The defense then took two more spades, but South had the rest for his contract.

Brilliant

"Brilliant play, partner," North marvelled.

"It sure was," East acknowledged. "If you follow with the deuce of spades at the first trick, I'll know my partner has only four spades, and we can't take enough spade tricks to beat you. I'll shift to the king of hearts, and we get a spade, three hearts and a club. As it was, I thought my partner had a five-card spade suit."

I'll say this for South: he thought faster at Trick 13 than at Trick One. "It was routine," he mumbled.

BIDDING QUIZ

You hold: ♠ A J 5 4 ♥ K Q 9 8 ♦ 9 7 6 ♣ K 5. Dealer, at your right, opens one spade. What do you say?

ANSWER: Pass. You'd double a one-club opening bid happily and a one-diamond opening less happily. Here, since you have good support for only one unbid suit, a double would be against the odds. Stay out of the auction and hope for a plus on defense.

```
Dlr: South          ♠ 9 7
Vul: N-S            ♥ J 4
                    ♦ Q J 5 3
                    ♣ A Q 10 7 3
♠ 10 8 6 3                          ♠ A J 5 4
♥ 10 6 3 2                          ♥ K Q 9 8
♦ 10 8 4                            ♦ 9 7 6
♣ 8 6                              ♣ K 5
                    ♠ K Q 2
                    ♥ A 7 5
                    ♦ A K 2
                    ♣ J 9 4 2
```

South	West	North	East
1 NT	Pass	3 NT	All Pass

Opening lead: ♠3

32.

Haste Costs Slam

You can't beat the deal below as a lesson in careful play to the first trick.

North-South reached a fine slam, with both players properly appreciating the value of their aces and kings. South was delighted with the trump opening lead; his guess for the queen was eliminated.

South played low from dummy and took East's queen with the ace. When declarer next led a trump to the king and saw the 4-1 break, however, his optimism waned. If he ruffed a spade with dummy's ten, West would get a trump trick. In fact, with the diamonds lying badly, the slam was no longer makable.

Spade Ruff

Since no West would lead from the queen of trumps against a slam, South should put up dummy's king at the first trick. He next takes the K-A of spades and ruffs a spade with the eight.

Inasmuch as East's queen of trumps fell at the first trick, South can then cash the ten of trumps, lead a club to the ace, draw trumps and try the diamond finesse for an overtrick.

If East follows with a low trump at the first trick, South finesses in trumps after ruffing a spade.

BIDDING QUIZ

You hold: ♠ Q 10 4 3 ♥ Q ♦ K 10 7 6 ♣ J 10 6 4. Your partner opens one heart, you respond one spade, and he next bids two clubs. The opponents pass. What do you say?

ANSWER: This situation is difficult, since opener could have as many as 17 points. Though you could miss game by passing, the chance of getting too high if you raise to three clubs is greater. Partner would surely go on, perhaps to 3NT, with about 15 points. Pass.

```
Dlr: North        ♠ K 7
Vul: N-S          ♥ K 10 8
                  ♦ A Q J 4
                  ♣ K 7 5 3
♠ J 8 6 5                        ♠ Q 10 4 3
♥ 9 7 6 4                        ♥ Q
♦ 9 8                            ♦ K 10 7 6
♣ Q 9 2                          ♣ J 10 6 4
                  ♠ A 9 2
                  ♥ A J 5 3 2
                  ♦ 5 3 2
                  ♣ A 8
```

North	East	South	West
1 NT	Pass	3♥	Pass
4♥	Pass	5♥	Pass
6♥	All Pass		

Opening lead: ♥4

33.

Dlr: South
Vul: None

♠ 7 4 3
♥ J 10 5
♦ A Q 7 5
♣ 7 6 4

♠ A K J 10 6
♥ A K 9 4
♦ 4 3
♣ K 9

South	West	North	East
1♠	Pass	2♠	Pass
4♠	All Pass		

West leads the ♦J, and dummy's queen loses to East's king. Back comes the ♣J, and West takes the ace and queen. You ruff the third club, go to the ♦A and lead the ♥J, which holds. The ♥10 also holds. How do you continue?

34.

Dlr: South
Vul: None

♠ J 7
♥ Q 5 3
♦ K 7 5 2
♣ K Q 6 3

♠ K 5 3
♥ A K
♦ Q J 4
♣ J 10 7 4 2

South	West	North	East
1♣	Dbl	Redbl	Pass
Pass	1♦	2♣	Pass
2 NT	Pass	3 NT	All Pass

West leads the ♥10. Plan the play.

35.

Dlr: South
Vul: N-S

♠ A Q 9 3
♥ K 6 4 2
♦ Q 7 2
♣ Q 4

♠ K J 10 7 4 2
♥ A J
♦ A 6 3
♣ A J

South	West	North	East
1♠	Pass	3♠	Pass
6♠	All Pass		

West leads the ♣10 to the queen, king and ace. How do you continue?

36.

Dlr: South
Vul: N-S

♠ Q 8 2
♥ Q J 3
♦ K 8 6 5 2
♣ K 3

```
       N
    W     E      ♠ 7 5 3
       S         ♥ A 10
                 ♦ A Q 10
                 ♣ J 8 7 5 2
```

South	West	North	East
1♠	Pass	2♦	Pass
2♠	Pass	3♠	Pass
4♠	All Pass		

West leads the ♥4 to dummy's queen and your ace. How do you continue?

33.

A Mythed Inference?

Few people know that one of antiquity's great conflicts, the Trojan War, began because of a bridge game.

The trouble started when Hector was declarer at four spades on the deal below. The Trojan prince played dummy's queen of diamonds at the first trick. Odysseus, East for the visiting Greeks, won the king and returned the jack of clubs. West, Achilles, took the ace and queen of clubs and led a third club.

Hector ruffed, got to dummy with the ace of diamonds, led the jack of hearts for a finesse and continued with the ten of hearts, which also won.

Top Honors

The kibitzers expected declarer to finesse in trumps next, but instead Hector went against the odds by cashing the A-K. When Achilles' queen dropped, the game was made.

Then, according to the ancient writings, Hector unwisely boasted of his acumen. "I knew it couldn't be right to finesse in trumps," he crowed. "The wily Odysseus would not have failed to cover the ten of hearts if he held the guarded queen of trumps. Beware of Greeks bearing entries to dummy."

Enraged by these artless remarks, Achilles promptly skewered South with his sword, and the fight was on; but Hector's last words (slightly altered) survive.

BIDDING QUIZ

You hold: ♠ Q 2 ♥ 8 7 ♦ J 10 9 2 ♣ A Q 8 5 3. Dealer, at your left, opens one diamond, and your partner doubles. The next player passes. What do you say?

ANSWER: Bid 1NT. You promise six to nine points with a trick in diamonds. Since a 1NT response aims toward the most likely game, it's better than a jump response in clubs. Actually, with your five-card suit, your hand is almost worth a game-invitational jump to 2NT.

```
Dlr: South          ♠ 7 4 3
Vul: None           ♥ J 10 5
                    ♦ A Q 7 5
                    ♣ 7 6 4

♠ Q 2                               ♠ 9 8 5
♥ 8 7                               ♥ Q 6 3 2
♦ J 10 9 2                          ♦ K 8 6
♣ A Q 8 5 3                         ♣ J 10 2

                    ♠ A K J 10 6
                    ♥ A K 9 4
                    ♦ 4 3
                    ♣ K 9
```

South	West	North	East
1♠	Pass	2♠	Pass
4♠	All Pass		

Opening lead: ♦J

34.

Finesse Couldn't Lose

If you're suffering through a drought of losing finesses, the remedy is simple: try a finesse that can't lose.

South won the first trick, thankful to have escaped a spade opening lead. He knew, though, that West would switch to spades when he regained the lead.

If South knocked out the ace of clubs early, he could count only eight tricks: one spade to come, four clubs and three hearts. To assure the contract, South needed to steal a diamond trick before shifting to clubs.

Sure Thing

To accomplish his goal, declarer dusted off an ancient tactic, the sure-thing finesse. At the second trick, he led the jack of diamonds.

West was caught on the hop. Reflexively, he followed with the three of diamonds, halfway expecting South to play low from dummy, and East to produce the queen. South, however, had taken a finesse that couldn't lose.

When the jack of diamonds won the trick, South hastily switched to clubs and ended with exactly nine tricks.

BIDDING QUIZ

You hold: ♠ K 5 3 ♥ A K ♦ Q J 4 ♣ J 10 7 4 2. You open one club, and partner responds one spade. You bid 1NT, and he tries three hearts. The opponents pass. What do you say?

ANSWER: Bid three spades. Partner, who is certain to have five or more spades, would like to know that your side has an eight-card fit. If your spades were slightly stronger, you could jump to four spades, but you can't support hearts with a doubleton — even the A-K.

Dlr: South	♠ J 7	
Vul: None	♥ Q 5 3	
	♦ K 7 5 2	
	♣ K Q 6 3	

♠ A Q 10 2		♠ 9 8 6 4
♥ 10 9 8 4		♥ J 7 6 2
♦ A 8 3		♦ 10 9 6
♣ A 5		♣ 9 8

	♠ K 5 3	
	♥ A K	
	♦ Q J 4	
	♣ J 10 7 4 2	

South	West	North	East
1♣	Dbl	Redbl	Pass
Pass	1♠	2♣	Pass
2 NT	Pass	3 NT	All Pass

Opening lead: ♥10

35.

Horseplay

Horsesense indicates the best play in the deal below, but South went down when he put the cart before the horse.

The hand was over quicker than a horserace. South took the first trick with the ace of clubs, drew trumps and finessed with the jack of hearts. Alas, his horseshoe had lost its magic. West won the queen and led a club. South then horsed around for a few tricks, but he finally lost horsepower. West let out a horselaugh as his king of diamonds took the setting trick.

"You backed the wrong horse," North complained. "It's a horse of a different color if you try diamonds first."

"Hold your horses," South protested. "I had eleven tricks; I needed one of two finesses for a twelfth. Get off your high horse and give me a break."

Dead Horse

You can lead a horse to water, North thought wearily, but...

"Not to beat a dead horse," he said, "but the play you chose was strictly horse-and-buggy. If you lead diamonds first, and my queen loses to the king, you still have a chance in hearts. But if you try an early heart finesse and it loses, you're down; you must lose a diamond."

"Horsefeathers!" muttered South, finally seeing the light.

With two chances for your contract, first try the one that won't leave you unhorsed if it fails. And that advice comes straight from — where else? — the horse's mouth.

BIDDING QUIZ

You hold: ♠ A Q 9 3 ♥ K 6 4 2 ♦ Q 7 2 ♣ Q 4. Your partner opens one diamond, you respond one heart, and he next bids two clubs. The opponents pass. What do you say?

ANSWER: Bid 3NT. Now that partner has bid twice, you must take the initiative and place the contract.

```
Dlr: South          ♠ A Q 9 3
Vul: N-S            ♥ K 6 4 2
                    ♦ Q 7 2
                    ♣ Q 4
♠ 8 5                               ♠ 6
♥ Q 8 7                             ♥ 10 9 5 3
♦ K 9 4                             ♦ J 10 8 5
♣ 10 9 8 6 3                        ♣ K 7 5 2
                    ♠ K J 10 7 4 2
                    ♥ A J
                    ♦ A 6 3
                    ♣ A J
```

South	West	North	East
1♠	Pass	3♠	Pass
6♠	All Pass		

Opening lead: ♣10

FRANK STEWART

36.

Help Your Partner

South in the deal below put up dummy's queen of hearts at the first trick. East won and hastily returned the ten of hearts to West's king. Declarer sneakily followed with the seven and eight. West then mulled over his next play, while East wondered what the problem was.

In fact, West was worried about the missing five of hearts. If South had it, West needed to lead another heart; if East had the five, a diamond shift was best. Eventually, West misguessed by leading a diamond, and South was able to make his contract.

Heart Return

"Why would I be so eager to return a heart if I had three of them?" East demanded.

"If declarer has two diamonds, two hearts and the A-Q-J-x of clubs, he'll make it if you don't," West glared. "He takes two trumps, throws dummy's hearts on the clubs, and ruffs a heart."

I blame East for the foulup. East can compel West to make the winning play by cashing the ace of diamonds before returning a heart. Yes, South might ruff; but then he will hold the top spades and clubs for his bidding, and the game will be unbeatable.

BIDDING QUIZ

You hold: ♠ 9 6 ♥ K 9 6 4 2 ♦ J 9 4 3 ♣ 9 4. Partner opens two hearts (strong), and the next player passes. What do you say?

ANSWER: Bid four hearts. A jump to game in response to a strong two-bid promises excellent trump support, but no side ace, king or singleton. With any of those features, you would raise to three hearts, leaving room for slam investigation. The actual response discourages slam.

```
Dlr: South            ♠ Q 8 2
Vul: N-S              ♥ Q J 3
                      ♦ K 8 6 5 2
                      ♣ K 3
♠ 9 6                                    ♠ 7 5 3
♥ K 9 6 4 2                              ♥ A 10
♦ J 9 4 3                                ♦ A Q 10
♣ 9 4                                    ♣ J 8 7 5 2
                      ♠ A K J 10 4
                      ♥ 8 7 5
                      ♦ 7
                      ♣ A Q 10 6
```

South	West	North	East
1♠	Pass	2♦	Pass
2♠	Pass	3♣	Pass
4♠	All Pass		

Opening lead: ♥4

37.

Dlr: West   ♠ K Q 9 5 3
Vul: Both   ♥ A Q J 5
       ♦ A K
       ♣ J 5

♠ A 10
♥ 4
♦ J 7 3
♣ A K 8 7 6 4 2

```
      N
   W     E
      S
```

West	North	East	South
1♣	Dbl	Pass	1♥
2♣	3♥	All Pass	

You cash two club tricks; South had the Q-9 doubleton. How do you continue?

38.

Dlr: South   ♠ K 4
Vul: N-S   ♥ Q 10 8 3
       ♦ 4 3
       ♣ A 10 9 5 2

       ♠ A 6 5 3
       ♥ 9 2
       ♦ A Q J 2
       ♣ K Q 4

South	West	North	East
1 NT	Pass	2♣	Pass
2♠	Pass	3 NT	All Pass

West leads the ♠Q. Plan the play.

39.

Dlr: North
Vul: N-S

♠ K 4 2
♥ A
♦ A Q J 10 6
♣ Q 7 6 3

♠ A J 10 9 3
♥ 7 6 5 4
♦ K 4 3
♣ 2

North	East	South	West
1♦	Pass	1♠	Pass
2♣	Pass	2♠	Pass
4♠	All Pass		

West leads the ♥Q. Plan the play.

40.

Dlr: West
Vul: N-S

♠ J 7 3
♥ Q J 8 4
♦ A Q 10 4
♣ A K

```
    N
  W   E
    S
```

♠ K
♥ 9 6 3
♦ 8 7 6 3
♣ 10 7 5 4 3

West	North	East	South
1♣	Dbl	Pass	2♠
Pass	3 NT	Pass	4♠
All Pass			

West leads the ♥K. Plan the defense.

37.

A Helpful Ruff-Sluff

West knew what terrible things can happen — during and after the play — to defenders who present declarer with a ruff-sluff. After West cashed the A-K of clubs, he therefore led a diamond.

South happily won dummy's ace and led the ace and another trump, losing to East's king. Declarer won the next diamond, drew trumps, conceded the ace of spades and claimed his contract.

West thought the defense had done its best, but East had other ideas.

Five Tricks

"We need five tricks," East began, "and you can see we'll get none in diamonds. You must assume that I have the king of trumps, but you can't count on me for K-10-x-x. To beat the contract for sure, we need a spade ruff. Your best chance is to lead another club at the third trick."

"But that gives declarer a ruff-sluff," West recoiled.

"It does him no good," East replied. "He has no losers to sluff. But it helps ME because I can throw a spade. When I win the king of trumps, I lead my last spade and get a ruff."

BIDDING QUIZ

You hold: ♠ 8 6 ♥ K 8 7 ♦ Q 10 9 6 5 4 ♣ 10 3. Your partner opens 1NT, and you respond two diamonds. Partner then bids 2NT. The opponents pass. What do you say?

ANSWER: Probably something unprintable. Partner should have passed two diamonds, respecting your signoff. Three diamonds may be a better contract than 2NT, but a partner who would bid 2NT over two diamonds is fully capable of bidding 3NT over three diamonds. Pass to avoid a big loss.

```
Dlr: West              ♠ K Q 9 5 3
Vul: Both              ♥ A Q J 5
                       ♦ A K
                       ♣ J 5
    ♠ A 10                            ♠ 8 6
    ♥ 4                               ♥ K 8 7
    ♦ J 7 3                           ♦ Q 10 9 6 5 4
    ♣ A K 8 7 6 4 2                   ♣ 10 3
                       ♠ J 7 4 2
                       ♥ 10 9 6 3 2
                       ♦ 8 2
                       ♣ Q 9
```

West	North	East	South
1♣	Dbl	Pass	1♥
2♣	3♥	All Pass	

Opening lead: ♣K

38.

Varied Approaches

This 3NT contract is easy to make if the clubs run, but then the deal wouldn't be here.

In a duplicate event, one South won the first spade with the ace and took the K-Q of clubs. When West discarded, declarer continued with a club to the ace and gave up a club trick. East returned a spade to dummy's king. South cashed the good club and led a diamond to the jack, but he couldn't get back to dummy for another diamond finesse. He won only eight tricks.

No Entry

Another South took the first trick with the king of spades and finessed in diamonds at Trick Two. He then cashed three high clubs, but couldn't concede a club profitably because dummy was fresh out of entries. Although South won a second diamond finesse, he also went down.

One South got home. He took the ace of spades at the first trick and led the K-Q of clubs. When West discarded, South overtook with the ace and finessed in diamonds.

South then led a club to the ten and East's jack, took the spade return in dummy, cashed a club and repeated the diamond finesse for nine tricks.

BIDDING QUIZ

You hold: ♠ 8 2 ♥ A J 7 ♦ K 10 9 8 ♣ J 8 7 6. Dealer, at your left, opens one heart, and your partner doubles. The next player passes. What do you say?

ANSWER: Since partner promises support for the unbid suits, a bid of two clubs or two diamonds could work. A bid of 1NT is better because it tells partner that you have six to nine points with hearts stopped. You might have no points at all to respond in a minor suit.

```
Dlr: South              ♠ K 4
Vul: N-S                ♥ Q 10 8 3
                        ♦ 4 3
                        ♣ A 10 9 5 2
♠ Q J 10 9 7                              ♠ 8 2
♥ K 6 5 4                                 ♥ A J 7
♦ 7 6 5                                   ♦ K 10 9 8
♣ 3                                       ♣ J 8 7 6
                        ♠ A 6 5 3
                        ♥ 9 2
                        ♦ A Q J 2
                        ♣ K Q 4
```

South	West	North	East
1 NT	Pass	2♣	Pass
2♠	Pass	3 NT	All Pass

Opening lead: ♠Q

39.

Finesses in Wonderland

"Do you know about two-way finesses for a missing queen, child?" inquired the Red Queen.

"Yes, your majesty," Alice answered politely. "When you can finesse against either opponent, clues from the bidding and play may help place the queen."

"No, no," said the Queen with a touch of asperity. "I mean a *real* two-way finesse. First you finesse one way, then you finesse the other." Since Alice knew that strange things can happen at bridge, she kept silent.

Second Trick

"On this deal," pressed the Queen, "what do you do as declarer at the second trick?" She displayed the deal below.

"I lead a spade to the jack," Alice replied.

"Fine," boomed the Queen. "It's all over if West wins, so he plays low. Now if you lead a spade to the king, planning another finesse against East, you can no longer make your game.

"The proper play at the third trick," the Queen finished, "especially if you respect West's defense, is to lead the ten of spades and take the finesse the other way!"

Never mind, Alice; I'll say it for you. Curiouser and curiouser!

BIDDING QUIZ

You hold: ♠ K 4 2 ♥ A ♦ A Q J 10 6 ♣ Q 7 6 3. You open one diamond, and your partner responds one spade. You bid two clubs, he returns to two diamonds. The opponents pass. What do you say?

ANSWER: Bid two spades. Partner's diamond preference promises at most nine points. If you bid again, you say game is still possible and promise about 17 points. (With more, you would jump at your second turn.) Partner should be able to place the contract.

```
Dlr: North          ♠ K 4 2
Vul: N-S            ♥ A
                    ♦ A Q J 10 6
                    ♣ Q 7 6 3
♠ Q 8 7 5                           ♠ 6
♥ Q J 10 8                          ♥ K 9 3 2
♦ 9 2                               ♦ 8 7 5
♣ K J 10                            ♣ A 9 8 5 4
                    ♠ A J 10 9 3
                    ♥ 7 6 5 4
                    ♦ K 4 3
                    ♣ 2
```

North	East	South	West
1♦	Pass	1♠	Pass
2♣	Pass	2♠	Pass
4♠	All Pass		

Opening lead: ♥Q

40.

Defense in Wonderland

"When I play a card," Humpty Dumpty told Alice loftily, "it means exactly what I want it to mean."

Defense is much easier if you sit on a wall. (Usually, you can see all four hands.) Still, Humpty Dumpty had just allowed the Mock Turtle to make a hopeless game.

When Alice led the king of hearts, the Egg, East, followed with the three. Alice then shifted to a diamond, and the Mock Turtle promptly stopped his sobbing. He took three diamonds to pitch his last heart and led a trump. Alice winced when East's king came up.

Signals Low

"When you signalled with a low heart, you egged me — sorry — into a losing shift," Alice grumbled at her partner. "What if you hold the king of diamonds instead of the king of spades? In this situation, to play low implies that you can stand a shift."

Alice was right. Since East knows that the defense needs two heart tricks and two trumps, he must signal with the nine of hearts at Trick One. All the king's horses and all the king's men can't help if a player forgets that the only purpose of a signal is to direct the defense.

BIDDING QUIZ

You hold: ♠ A 8 ♥ A K 5 2 ♦ 9 5 2 ♣ Q 8 6 2. Your partner opens one diamond, you respond one heart, and he next bids one spade. The opponents pass. What do you say?

ANSWER: The best contract is unclear. A bid of 2NT isn't forcing, and you want to reach game. A leap to 3NT may land you in the wrong spot; your partner could be short in clubs. Mark time with a bid of two clubs and let him describe his hand further.

```
Dlr: West          ♠ J 7 3
Vul: N-S           ♥ Q J 8 4
                   ♦ A Q 10 4
                   ♣ A K

♠ A 8                          ♠ K
♥ A K 5 2                      ♥ 9 6 3
♦ 9 5 2                        ♦ 8 7 6 3
♣ Q 8 6 2                      ♣ 10 7 5 4 3

                   ♠ Q 10 9 6 5 4 2
                   ♥ 10 7
                   ♦ K J
                   ♣ J 9
```

West	North	East	South
1♣	Dbl	Pass	2♠
Pass	3 NT	Pass	4♠
All Pass			

Opening lead: ♥K

41.

Dlr: South
Vul: N-S

     ♠ Q 10 6
     ♥ 5 3
     ♦ 10 9 7 3
     ♣ A K 10 3

     ♠ J 9 7
     ♥ A K
     ♦ A K J 8
     ♣ J 5 4 2

South	West	North	East
1 NT	Pass	3 NT	All Pass

West leads the ♣4, and dummy's queen holds. East plays the two. How do you continue?

42.

Dlr: North
Vul: Both

     ♠ K 10 5 2
     ♥ A Q
     ♦ K 8 3
     ♣ Q 7 4 2

     ♠ A Q J 9 4 3
     ♥ J 8 4
     ♦ 9 6 4
     ♣ 5

North	East	South	West
1♣	Pass	1♠	2♦
2♠	Pass	3♠	Pass
4♠	All Pass		

West leads the ♥2. Plan the play.

43.

♠ 7 6 4
♥ Q 8 7 5
♦ J 4
♣ A 9 5 2

South	West	North	East
1♠	Pass	2♦	Pass
2♠	Pass	3♥	Pass
4♠	Pass	5♠	All Pass

What should West lead?

44.

Dlr: South
Vul: N-S

♠ J 9 3
♥ A K 4
♦ A K J 10 3
♣ K 2

♠ K 10 5
♥ Q J 3
♦ Q 5
♣ A J 5 4 3

South	West	North	East
1♣	Pass	2♦	Pass
2 NT	Pass	6 NT	All Pass

West leads the ♥10. Plan the play.

41.

Beware Criticism

Bad-mouthing your partner's play right at the table may backfire. Your off-the-cuff analysis may be off the mark.

South won the first spade in dummy and saw that a winning finesse in a minor suit would give him nine tricks. He therefore passed the ten of diamonds at the second trick.

West took his queen, cashed three spade tricks and led a heart. South won and tried a club finesse with dummy's ten. This time his luck was in, and 3NT scraped home.

Top Clubs

North shook his head. "You would go down if the opening leader had five spades," he complained. "Give yourself an extra chance. Before you finesse in diamonds, cash the A-K of clubs. If the queen falls, you don't need the diamond finesse."

South's play was wrong, but so was North's impulsive critique. At the second trick, South should lead a spade!

If West can cash only three spades, South tries finesses in both minor suits — his best percentage play. But if West started with five spades and takes four spade tricks, South discards two diamonds from dummy and two clubs from his hand. When he regains the lead, he should cash the A-K of clubs, then finesse in diamonds if necessary.

BIDDING QUIZ

You hold: ♠ Q 10 6 ♥ 5 3 ♦ 10 9 7 3 ♣ A K 10 3. Your partner opens one club, you raise to two clubs, and he next bids 2NT. The opponents pass. What do you say?

ANSWER: Partner is interested in game; otherwise, he would pass you at two clubs. (He may have opened a "short club," but that alone wouldn't induce him to bid again after a raise.) Since you have a super-maximum, accept partner's invitation. Bid 3NT.

```
Dir: South          ♠ Q 10 6
Vul: N-S            ♥ 5 3
                    ♦ 10 9 7 3
                    ♣ A K 10 3
   ♠ A K 8 4                      ♠ 5 3 2
   ♥ J 9 4 2                      ♥ Q 10 8 7 6
   ♦ Q 2                          ♦ 6 5 4
   ♣ Q 7 6                        ♣ 9 8
                    ♠ J 9 7
                    ♥ A K
                    ♦ A K J 8
                    ♣ J 5 4 2
```

South	West	North	East
1 NT	Pass	3 NT	All Pass

Opening lead: ♠4

FRANK STEWART

42.

Looking Ahead

The play often starts before the auction ends. As the bidding unfolds, a good player will place cards around the table and visualize how the play will go. Thus, when North in the deal below bid game, he was giving West the ace of diamonds.

Unfortunately, North planned the play better than did South, the declarer. South finessed with the queen of hearts at the first trick. East won the king and shifted promptly to the jack of diamonds. West took the ace and returned the ten to let East ruff dummy's king. East then led a club, and West won the ace and cashed the queen of diamonds. Down two.

No Gain

South cannot win more than two heart tricks in any event, but the consequences of losing a finesse at the first trick are clear; West probably has six-card diamond suit for his overcall.

South should take the ace of hearts, draw trumps and give up a heart to the king. If the defenders force out dummy's king of diamonds, South gets to his hand with a trump and throws a diamond on the jack of hearts. A diamond ruff in dummy is his tenth trick.

BIDDING QUIZ

You hold: ♠ 8 6 ♥ K 10 7 6 3 ♦ J ♣ K 10 9 6 3. Your partner opens one diamond, you respond one heart, and he next bids one spade. The opponents pass. What do you say?

ANSWER: You have few choices. A cautious pass, though it assures at worst a small minus, is presumptuous. A bid of two clubs fails to limit your strength; partner might then bid too much. Try 1NT even though you would prefer balanced distribution.

```
Dlr: North        ♠ K 10 5 2
Vul: Both         ♥ A Q
                  ♦ K 8 3
                  ♣ Q 7 4 2
♠ 7                               ♠ 8 6
♥ 9 5 2                           ♥ K 10 7 6 3
♦ A Q 10 7 5 2                    ♦ J
♣ A J 8                           ♣ K 10 9 6 3
                  ♠ A Q J 9 4 3
                  ♥ J 8 4
                  ♦ 9 6 4
                  ♣ 5
```

North	East	South	West
1♣	Pass	1♠	2♦
2♠	Pass	3♠	Pass
4♠	All Pass		

Opening lead: ♥2

43.

Look at the Road Map

Some auctions are more revealing than others. If your opponents bid one spade-three spades-six spades, they may have no idea whether the slam will be a good one, but they know you must make the opening lead in the dark. A slow, careful auction may be more accurate, but it may also draw the defenders a road map.

In the deal below, North-South stopped delicately at five spades. West, having heard his opponents bid every other suit, nodded knowingly and laid down the ace of clubs at the first trick. Another club went to East's king, but that was all for the defense; South made game and rubber.

Club Control

West can defeat the contract if he looks at his complimentary road map. North-South were clearly in search of slam. North's bidding suggested that he had everything under control except clubs; South's final pass admitted that he had no club help. West can thus place East with the king of clubs.

Underleading aces against suit contracts is usually a risky business, but not here. If West leads a low club at Trick One, East wins and returns a club to the ace. A third club lead then gives East a ruff to defeat the contract and may convince North-South to employ a more direct approach in the bidding next time.

BIDDING QUIZ

You hold: ♠ Q ♥ A J 4 ♦ A K Q 6 3 ♣ Q 8 7 3. You open one diamond, and your partner responds one spade. The opponents pass. What do you say?

ANSWER: Bid two clubs. Your hand is not quite strong enough for a jump to three clubs, which would force to game even if partner had only six points (a minimum response). Though you have 18 points, the unguarded queen of spades is worth less than usual. If partner keeps the bidding alive, you can bid strongly later.

```
Dlr: East           ♠ Q
Vul: Both           ♥ A J 4
                    ♦ A K Q 6 3
                    ♣ Q 8 7 3
♠ 7 6 4                             ♠ 8 2
♥ Q 8 7 5                           ♥ 10 9 3 2
♦ J 4                               ♦ 10 9 8 7 5
♣ A 9 5 2                           ♣ K 6
                    ♠ A K J 10 9 5 3
                    ♥ K 6
                    ♦ 2
                    ♣ J 10 4
```

South	West	North	East
1♠	Pass	2♦	Pass
2♠	Pass	3♥	Pass
4♠	Pass	5♠	All Pass

Opening lead: ??

44.

Big Brother on Bridge

All finesses are equal; every one is a 50-50 proposition. But good players know when one finesse is vastly more equal than another.

South took the first trick in dummy and saw a chance to win all 13 tricks. He therefore cashed the king of clubs and led a club for an ill-fated finesse with the jack. When West won the queen, he lost no time in laying down the ace of spades. Down one.

Not Assured

It's clear that declarer can succeed by finessing against the queen of spades at the second trick. Although a club finesse will work as often as a spade finesse, South forgot that slam isn't assured even if the club finesse wins. (South must still guess whether to play for a 3-3 club split or try for a spade trick.)

A spade finesse is also better because if West wins the queen, the defense may not cash the ace of spades. Given a chance, South can try the clubs.

Always count your tricks as declarer; maybe you can spot the "equalest" finesse. And maybe I should've written up this deal in 1984. Or, well ... maybe not.

BIDDING QUIZ

You hold: ♠ A 8 6 2 ♥ 10 9 8 2 ♦ 6 4 2 ♣ Q 7. Your partner opens one diamond, you respond one heart, and he next bids one spade. The opponents pass. What do you say?

ANSWER: Pass. Partner did not jump to two spades, which would promise at least 19 points and force your side to game. Since the value of your queen of clubs is questionable, and you have a terrible holding in partner's first suit, game looks impossible.

```
Dlr: South          ♠ J 9 3
Vul: N-S            ♥ A K 4
                    ♦ A K J 10 3
                    ♣ K 2
♠ A 8 6 2                           ♠ Q 7 4
♥ 10 9 8 2                          ♥ 7 6 5
♦ 6 4 2                             ♦ 9 8 7
♣ Q 7                               ♣ 10 9 8 6
                    ♠ K 10 5
                    ♥ Q J 3
                    ♦ Q 5
                    ♣ A J 5 4 3
```

South	West	North	East
1♣	Pass	2♦	Pass
2 NT	Pass	6 NT	All Pass

Opening lead: ♥10

45.

Dlr: North		♠ K 7 3	
Vul: N-S		♥ 8 5 3	
		♦ A K Q 10 8 3	
		♣ J	

	♠ A Q 5
	♥ K 7 4
	♦ 6 2
	♣ Q 10 8 6 2

North	East	South	West
1♦	Dbl	Redbl	Pass
Pass	2♣	Dbl	2♥
Pass	Pass	2 NT	Pass
Pass	3 NT	All Pass	

West leads the ♥6. East wins the ace and returns the ♥2. Plan the play.

46.

Dlr: South		♠ K 6	
Vul: None		♥ Q J 4	
		♦ 9 6 3	
		♣ A 8 5 4 3	

	♠ Q 8
	♥ A K 10 7 2
	♦ K 10
	♣ Q J 7 2

South	West	North	East
1♥	3♠	4♥	All Pass

West leads the ♦J. East wins the ace and returns a diamond. West ruffs your king, cashes the ♠A and leads another spade. East follows with the ten and deuce, and dummy's king wins. It takes three rounds to draw trumps, East having started with a singleton. How do you play the clubs?

FRANK STEWART

47.

Dlr: South ♠ K 6 4 3 2
Vul: Both   ♥ K 7
            ♦ 4
            ♣ 9 6 4 3 2

            ♠ 7 5
            ♥ Q J 10 9 8
            ♦ A 7 5 3
            ♣ A Q

South	West	North	East
1♥	Pass	1♠	Pass
2♦	Pass	2♥	All Pass

West leads the ♦Q. Plan the play.

48.

Dlr: South ♠ 8 6 4 2
Vul: N-S   ♥ A 10 9 3
            ♦ 4 2
            ♣ 7 5 3

            ♠ K Q 3
            ♥ 6 4 2
            ♦ A K 7 5
            ♣ A K Q

South	West	North	East
2 NT	Pass	3♣	Pass
3♦	Pass	3 NT	All Pass

West leads the ♠5. East wins the ace and returns the ♠J to
your queen. When you lead a heart, West plays the jack, you
duck, and East follows with the eight. Another spade goes to
your king, and you lead a second heart: queen from West,
nine, seven. West cashes the ♠10 and leads a low heart. Do
you finesse with dummy's ten or put up the ace?

45.

Remarkable Finesse

South in the deal below wins my Finesse of the Year Award. His opponents were ready to nominate him for something else — until he explained his play.

East took the first trick with the ace of hearts and returned the deuce. South won the third heart and, after a modest pause, led a diamond for a finesse with dummy's eight! East's eyebrows went into orbit, and West grumbled about people who play a little too well.

South then got to his hand with a spade, finessed with the ten of diamonds, and took ten tricks with high diamonds and spades.

Analysis

The defenders were still muttering when South offered his analysis. "If you" — he turned to West — "had a four-card major, you'd surely bid it over the redouble. And I doubt that you would run from two clubs doubled if you had three clubs.

"You" — he faced East — "led the deuce of hearts at the second trick, suggesting a four-card suit. So I gave you four spades, four hearts and five clubs.

"I may not be the world's greatest player," South finished, "but I can count to thirteen."

BIDDING QUIZ

You hold: ♠ K 7 3 ♥ 8 5 3 ♦ A K Q 10 8 3 ♣ J. Your partner opens one club, you respond one diamond, and he next bids 1NT. The opponents pass. What do you say?

ANSWER: Bid 3NT. Resist the temptation to rebid diamonds. When you table your dummy at notrump, partner will be charmed to see six probable tricks in diamonds. Except in an extreme case, which this is not, prefer the nine-trick game to an 11-trick game in a minor suit.

```
Dlr: North          ♠ K 7 3
Vul: N-S            ♥ 8 5 3
                    ♦ A K Q 10 8 3
                    ♣ J

♠ 9 4 2                           ♠ J 10 8 6
♥ Q 10 6                          ♥ A J 9 2
♦ J 9 7 5 4                       ♦ None
♣ 5 4                             ♣ A K 9 7 3

                    ♠ A Q 5
                    ♥ K 7 4
                    ♦ 6 2
                    ♣ Q 10 8 6 2
```

North	East	South	West
1♦	Dbl	Redbl	Pass
Pass	2♣	Dbl	2♥
Pass	Pass	2 NT	Pass
3 NT	All Pass		

Opening lead: ♥6

FRANK STEWART

46.

Count the Hand

The play South adopted in the deal below could have worked. All South needed was for West to have (the admittedly rare) 7-4-1-2 distribution.

East won the first trick with the ace of diamonds and returned a diamond. West ruffed and led the ace and a low spade. East followed with the ten and deuce.

After winning the king of spades, South drew trumps and led the queen of clubs for a finesse. Although West's king duly came forth, East still had the 10-9 of clubs to win a trick and defeat the contract.

Had Information

After South drew trumps, he had the necessary information to make the contract. West, who had preempted at the level of three, surely had a seven-card suit. (East's high-low play on the spade lead was supporting evidence.) West was also known to have started with a singleton diamond and four trumps.

Thus, unless West had been dealt 14 cards, there was room in his hand for only one club. South should thus have attacked clubs by leading low from his hand. The only chance to make game was that West's singleton club was the king.

BIDDING QUIZ

You hold: ♠ 10 2 ♥ 8 ♦ A Q 8 7 5 4 2 ♣ 10 9 6. You open three diamonds, and your partner bids 3NT. The opponents pass. What do you say?

ANSWER: Partner knows your hand. He has either diamond help and can run your suit, or he has a suit of his own and expects to take nine tricks without the diamonds. Since you have an ace (your diamonds might have been headed by K-J or worse), you can pass with confidence.

```
Dlr: South          ♠ K 6
Vul: None           ♥ Q J 4
                    ♦ 9 6 3
                    ♣ A 8 5 4 3
  ♠ A J 9 7 5 4 3                    ♠ 10 2
  ♥ 9 6 5 3                          ♥ 8
  ♦ J                                ♦ A Q 8 7 5 4 2
  ♣ K                                ♣ 10 9 6
                    ♠ Q 8
                    ♥ A K 10 7 2
                    ♦ K 10
                    ♣ Q J 7 2
```

South	West	North	East
1♥	3♠	4♥	All Pass

Opening lead: ♦J

47.

Sins Kill Contract

A reassuring aspect of bridge is that sins often go unpunished. West in the deal below was washed clean; South wasn't as lucky.

Since West had strong diamonds and general strength, his proper opening lead was a trump. North had shown a preference for hearts, and diamond ruffs in dummy were imminent.

I don't envy West his actual choice, the queen of diamonds, but he survived when South lusted after overtricks. South won the ace, ruffed a diamond and slothfully finessed with the queen of clubs. When West won the king, he drew dummy's remaining trump, and the defense took two spades and two diamonds. Down one.

Ranks High

Though West's opening lead was only a mild transgression, South's play ranks right up there alongside covetousness, anger and pride. After the first trick, South has four heart tricks, a diamond and a club. Two diamond ruffs will make his total eight.

After ruffing one diamond, South must not be a glutton. He should lead a club to his ace and ruff a second diamond to assure his contract.

BIDDING QUIZ

You hold: ♠ 7 5 ♥ Q J 10 9 8 ♦ A 7 5 3 ♣ A Q. Your partner opens 1NT, you respond three hearts, and he next bids three spades. The opponents pass. What do you say?

ANSWER: Partner has heart support; else, he would return to 3NT. If partner had an average hand with fair support, he would raise to four hearts. He actually promises a maximum hand with excellent support. Cooperate in the slam hunt by cue-bidding four clubs.

Dlr: South	♠ K 6 4 3 2	
Vul: Both	♥ K 7	
	♦ 4	
	♣ 9 6 4 3 2	

♠ Q 9 8		♠ A J 10
♥ A 6 4 2		♥ 5 3
♦ Q J 10 2		♦ K 9 8 6
♣ K 5		♣ J 10 8 7

	♠ 7 5	
	♥ Q J 10 9 8	
	♦ A 7 5 3	
	♣ A Q	

South	West	North	East
1♥	Pass	1♠	Pass
2♦	Pass	2♥	All Pass

Opening lead: ♦Q

48.

Courting Trouble

"Your honor," intoned the District Attorney, "we will prove that South, the defendant, lost his contract of three notrump due to poor play."

"The court will kibitz the evidence," came the ruling from the bench, and the D.A. presented his case.

East took the ace of spades at the first trick and returned the jack. South won and led a heart. West put up the jack, and South played low, preserving a link with dummy; East played the eight of hearts. South won the next spade and led another heart: queen from West, nine, seven.

No Tricks

After cashing the ten of spades, West led his last heart. South then finessed with dummy's ten and wound up with no heart tricks at all.

"My client was merely unlucky," defense counsel contended. "How could he know, especially when East signalled high-low in hearts, that the suit would split three-three?"

"Guilty," pronounced the judge. "Declarer should have gone up with dummy's ace on the third heart. Did the defendant think that West would start a spade from 10-9-7-5 on opening lead if he held K-Q-J-5 in hearts?"

BIDDING QUIZ

You hold: ♠ 8 6 4 2 ♥ A 10 9 3 ♦ 4 2 ♣ 7 5 3. Dealer, at your left, opens one heart. Your partner doubles, and the next player passes. What do you say?

ANSWER: Take out the double; bid one spade. Nothing bad will happen; partner has either spades or a strong hand with a suit of his own. A contract of one heart doubled might make easily. You need better hearts to convert the double to penalty by passing.

```
Dlr: South          ♠ 8 6 4 2
Vul: N-S            ♥ A 10 9 3
                    ♦ 4 2
                    ♣ 7 5 3
♠ 10 9 7 5                        ♠ A J
♥ Q J 5                           ♥ K 8 7
♦ J 9 3                           ♦ Q 10 8 6
♣ J 4 2                           ♣ 10 9 8 6
                    ♠ K Q 3
                    ♥ 6 4 2
                    ♦ A K 7 5
                    ♣ A K Q
```

South	West	North	East
2 NT	Pass	3♣	Pass
3♦	Pass	3 NT	All Pass

Opening lead: ♠5

49.

♠ A 8 5 3
♥ K 10 8 6 3
♦ 8 2
♣ 8 3

South	West	North	East
1♠	Pass	2♠	Pass
4♠	All Pass		

What should West lead?

50.

Dlr: North   ♠ A K J 10 5
Vul: None   ♥ 3
                  ♦ A K
                  ♣ Q 8 6 5 2

                              ♠ Q 6 2
                              ♥ K 9 6 5
        N   ♦ 10 8 3
     W   E   ♣ K J 3
        S

North	East	South	West
1♠	Pass	2♣	Pass
4♣	Pass	4♥	Pass
5 NT	Pass	6♣	All Pass

West leads the ♠3. Plan your defense.

51.

Dlr: South   ♠ K 10 4
Vul: N-S   ♥ J
                   ♦ 7 5 2
                   ♣ K Q J 9 7 4

```
            N              ♠ A 5 2
        W       E          ♥ K 9 7 5
            S              ♦ 9 8 4
                           ♣ A 8 3
```

South	West	North	East
1♠	Pass	2♣	Pass
2 NT	Pass	3♠	Pass
4♠	All Pass		

West leads the ♣2, and dummy plays the king. How do you defend?

52.

Dlr: South   ♠ J 9 7 3
Vul: Both   ♥ J 4
                   ♦ Q 9 7 4
                   ♣ A 6 3

                   ♠ A K Q 10 5 2
                   ♥ None
                   ♦ A 10 6 2
                   ♣ 8 5 2

South	West	North	East
1♠	2♥	2♠	3♥
4♠	All Pass		

West leads the ♥K. Can South guarantee his contract?

49.

Needed: A Strategy

Let's watch a poor defender handle the West cards in the deal below.

First, having been taught never to lead from kings, he starts with a club at the first trick. South wins the king and tables the king of spades. West grabs his ace and leads his other club "through strength."

South happily throws a heart on the ace of clubs, draws trumps and runs the diamonds for an overtrick. West goes on to the next deal, serenely unaware that he has chucked the defense.

Bother

A better West concentrates not on "rules," but on finding a way to beat the contract. He devises a strategy and launches it at the first trick. West's four trumps may be a bother to South, especially if South is forced to ruff once or twice. West therefore leads a heart, the suit in which South is most likely to be short.

South ruffs the third heart and leads a trump. If West wins, declarer can ruff the next heart in dummy, keeping three trumps in his hand to draw trumps.

West therefore refuses the first two trump leads. South will then go down whatever he does next.

BIDDING QUIZ

You hold: ♠ A 8 5 3 ♥ K 10 8 6 3 ♦ 8 2 ♣ 8 3. Your partner opens one diamond, you respond one heart, and he next bids two clubs. The opponents pass. What do you say?

ANSWER: Your best call may be one borrowed from chess: "Resign". A rebid of two hearts risks playing right there opposite a singleton. Two spades is sure to get you too high. Since partner should hold at least five diamonds, a false preference to two diamonds is the least evil.

```
Dlr: South          ♠ J 10 2
Vul: N-S            ♥ J 7 5
                    ♦ J 7 5
                    ♣ A J 10 6
♠ A 8 5 3                        ♠ 6
♥ K 10 8 6 3                     ♥ A Q 9
♦ 8 2                            ♦ 10 6 4
♣ 8 3                            ♣ Q 9 7 5 4 2
                    ♠ K Q 9 7 4
                    ♥ 4 2
                    ♦ A K Q 9 3
                    ♣ K
```

South	West	North	East
1♠	Pass	2♠	Pass
4♠	All Pass		

Opening lead: ??

FRANK STEWART

50.

Twist in the Tale

The play of the deal below has a surprise ending. How did expert South lose his slam?

North's bid of 5NT was the Grand Slam Force, a time-honored gadget that asked South to bid a grand slam with two top honors in trumps. When South couldn't oblige, the partnership stopped correctly at six clubs.

A poor declarer would have no trouble going down. With visions of 13 tricks, he would lead a club to the ace at the second trick, and West's discard would be like a splash of ice water.

Safety Play

The actual South knew his safety plays. He was ready to lead a club from dummy and insert the ten if East followed low. If West could win, declarer would later draw trumps with the ace and claim.

East, knowing what was about to happen, desperately sought a way to protect his trump holding. When South took the first trick with the ace of spades, East dropped the queen!

Now South didn't dare use his safety play. If West won a trick in trumps, East might get a spade ruff. So South led a trump straight to the ace, and down he went.

BIDDING QUIZ

You hold: ♠ 9 8 ♥ A J 7 ♦ Q 5 2 ♣ A 10 9 7 4. Dealer, at your left, opens one heart, and the next two players pass. What do you say?

ANSWER: Partner surely has a few points and may have as much as an opening bid. Don't let the opponents play in comfort when your side probably has a partscore or perhaps a game available. Balance with 1NT (which promises 10 to 14 points in this position) or two clubs.

Dlr: North	♠ A K J 10 5	
Vul: None	♥ 3	
	♦ A K	
	♣ Q 8 6 5 2	

♠ 7 4 3		♠ Q 6 2
♥ Q 10 8 4 2		♥ K 9 6 5
♦ J 9 7 6 4		♦ 10 8 3
♣ None		♣ K J 3

	♠ 9 8	
	♥ A J 7	
	♦ Q 5 2	
	♣ A 10 9 7 4	

North	East	South	West
1♠	Pass	2♣	Pass
4♣	Pass	4♥	Pass
5 NT	Pass	6♣	All Pass

Opening lead: ♠3

51.

Follow the Turtle

"Behold the turtle," goes the saying. "He progresses only when he sticks his neck out."

East in the deal below took the ace of clubs and withdrew into his shell to consider his next play. Since the opening lead was an obvious singleton, East feared for his life if he failed to give West a ruff. He thus returned a club.

West ruffed and led from the king of diamonds; since dummy's clubs were established, West had nothing to lose. South won the jack and led a trump. East took his ace and led another club. When West was unable to ruff, South was home.

Crucial

East's play doesn't matter if West has an ace; East's play is crucial when West has the king of diamonds. Then a diamond lead must come through South's A-Q, setting up the king before South can draw trumps and discard his diamonds on the clubs.

East should stick out his neck by leading a diamond at the second trick. Since East has the ace of trumps, he can wait to give West a club ruff. Although West may momentarily feel like making turtle soup out of East, he'll relent. Only the diamond return beats the contract.

BIDDING QUIZ

You hold: ♠ A 5 2 ♥ K 9 7 5 ♦ 9 8 4 ♣ A 8 3. Your partner opens one club, you respond one heart, and he rebids two clubs. The opponents pass. What do you say?

ANSWER: You must bid again with your 11 points, since game is possible. Raise to three clubs. Partner can pass with a bare minimum opening, but should bid on if he has a "maximum minimum" with about 15 points. If partner next bids three diamonds, for instance, you'll try 3NT.

```
Dlr: South          ♠ K 10 4
Vul: N-S            ♥ J
                    ♦ 7 5 2
                    ♣ K Q J 9 7 4
♠ 7 6                                    ♠ A 5 2
♥ Q 8 6 4 3 2                            ♥ K 9 7 5
♦ K 10 6 3                               ♦ 9 8 4
♣ 2                                      ♣ A 8 3
                    ♠ Q J 9 8 3
                    ♥ A 10
                    ♦ A Q J
                    ♣ 10 6 5
```

South	West	North	East
1♠	Pass	2♣	Pass
2 NT	Pass	3♠	Pass
4♠	All Pass		

Opening lead: ♣2

52.

True or False?

True or false? South can make sure of his game on the deal below no matter how the East-West cards lie.

The actual South showed that it was possible to go down. He ruffed the first trick, drew trumps, and led the ace and a low diamond. When West played low, declarer tried a finesse with dummy's nine. East won the jack, and South couldn't help losing two club tricks and another diamond.

Endplay

Since South has extra trumps, he can aim for an endplay. After drawing trumps, he ruffs dummy's last heart, takes the ace of clubs and gives the defense two club tricks.

If either defender then shifts to a diamond, South plays second hand low and loses only one diamond trick. If a defender instead leads a spade or club, giving up a ruff-sluff, South ruffs in dummy and throws a diamond from his hand. He then leads the queen of diamonds and plays low from his hand. Even if West could win the king, he would have to return a diamond into the A-10 or yield another ruff-sluff.

So the answer is "True"; best play guarantees the contract.

BIDDING QUIZ

You hold: ♠ 8 4 ♥ Q 9 8 6 2 ♦ K J 5 ♣ Q J 4. Dealer, at your left, opens one diamond, and your partner doubles. The next player passes. What do you say?

ANSWER: If your opponent had opened one spade, all of your high cards would be useful; you would jump to three hearts to invite game. As it is, your diamond honors sit in front of the opening bidder and are probably worthless. A response of one heart is enough.

Dlr: South	♠ J 9 7 3		
Vul: Both	♥ J 4		
	♦ Q 9 7 4		
	♣ A 6 3		
♠ 6			♠ 8 4
♥ A K 10 7 5 3			♥ Q 9 8 6 2
♦ 8 3			♦ K J 5
♣ K 10 9 7			♣ Q J 4
	♠ A K Q 10 5 2		
	♥ None		
	♦ A 10 6 2		
	♣ 8 5 2		

South	West	North	East
1♠	2♥	2♠	3♥
4♠	All Pass		

Opening lead: ♥K

53.

Dlr: South
Vul: N-S

♠ A 9 6
♥ Q J 2
♦ K 9 5 2
♣ 10 7 3

♠ K 7 5 2
♥ 4
♦ A 10 6 4 3
♣ A K Q

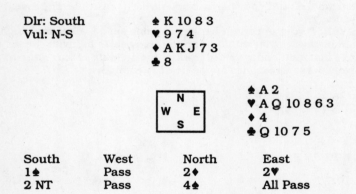

South	West	North	East
1♥	Dbl	Redbl	Pass
2♥	Dbl	3♥	Pass
4♥	All Pass		

You lead the ♣K and continue with the queen and ace, everyone following. What is your next play?

54.

Dlr: South
Vul: N-S

♠ K 10 8 3
♥ 9 7 4
♦ A K J 7 3
♣ 8

♠ A 2
♥ A Q 10 8 6 3
♦ 4
♣ Q 10 7 5

South	West	North	East
1♠	Pass	2♦	2♥
2 NT	Pass	4♠	All Pass

West leads the ♥2, and South plays the five under your ace.
How do you continue?

55.

Dlr: South		♠ J 5	
Vul: N-S		♥ 9 8 3	
		♦ A J 8 4	
		♣ A Q 10 9	

♠ None
♥ A K 10 7 5 2
♦ K 7 5 3 2
♣ K 2

South	West	North	East
1♥	Pass	2♣	Pass
2♦	Pass	3♥	Pass
4♦	Pass	5♣	Pass
6♥	All Pass		

West leads the ♠10. You ruff East's ace and cash the A-K of trumps, on which East throws a spade. You lead a third trump to West's queen and ruff the ♠K return. Next, you cash the top clubs and ruff a club; East had J-x-x-x. How do you play the diamonds?

56.

Dlr: South		♠ A Q 10 3	
Vul: N-S		♥ K 10 5 4	
		♦ A Q 3	
		♣ 9 2	

♠ K 4
♥ A J 6 3
♦ K J 8 2
♣ A 7 3

South	West	North	East
1 NT	Pass	2♣	Pass
2♥	Pass	5♥	Pass
6♥	All Pass		

West leads the ♣Q. Plan the play.

53.

When to Go Passive

West in the deal below cashed the three top clubs and sighed heavily when South followed suit.

"I knew I should've doubled four hearts," West said. He then laid down the ace of diamonds apologetically.

South pounced with a trump (opponents who reach game with only 21 high-card points turn up with void suits disturbingly often). He then drew trumps and led the queen of spades. West covered with the king, and it was all over. Declarer threw his low spade on the king of diamonds and claimed his contract.

Could Be Worse

"It might have been worse," East told West uncharitably. "You might have doubled."

West was too eager to snatch the setting trick. If South has a diamond loser, he can never avoid it; dummy has nothing South can use for a discard. But if South is void in diamonds, the king may provide him with a crucial discard for a spade loser.

At the fourth trick, West should exit passively with a trump, giving nothing away. Since East guards the third round of spades, South must lose a spade trick in the end and go down.

BIDDING QUIZ

You hold: ♠ 10 8 3 ♥ 9 7 6 ♦ Q J 8 7 ♣ 8 5 2. Dealer, at your left, opens one club. Your partner doubles, and the next player redoubles. What do you say?

ANSWER: Bid one diamond, which promises no points whatever, but suggests a safe port in the storm. If you pass, partner may run to an inferior contract in a major suit. A response of one diamond may also help partner find the best opening lead if the opponents play the hand.

```
Dlr: South        ♠ A 9 6
Vul: N-S          ♥ Q J 2
                  ♦ K 9 5 2
                  ♣ 10 7 3

♠ K 7 5 2                      ♠ 10 8 3
♥ 4                            ♥ 9 7 6
♦ A 10 6 4 3                   ♦ Q J 8 7
♣ A K Q                        ♣ 8 5 2

                  ♠ Q J 4
                  ♥ A K 10 8 5 3
                  ♦ None
                  ♣ J 9 6 4
```

South	West	North	East
1♥	Dbl	Redbl	Pass
2♥	Dbl	3♥	Pass
4♥	All Pass		

Opening lead: ♣K

FRANK STEWART

54.

Count the Tricks

Because South had bid 2NT, East easily diagnosed the opening heart lead as a singleton. East therefore took the ace of hearts at the first trick and fired back a heart for West to ruff.

This line of defense had only one flaw: it could not defeat the contract. South won West's diamond return and took the precaution (unnecessary, as it happened) of cashing the A-K of clubs to discard dummy's last heart before he led a trump. East's ace of trumps was the last trick for the defense, and South made his game.

Obvious Tricks

Before plunging ahead, East should count his defensive tricks. The major-suit aces and a heart ruff are obvious tricks, but unless West miraculously holds the ace of clubs, the setting trick must be a diamond ruff.

At the second trick, East should lead the four of diamonds. Since East has control of trumps, West's heart ruff can wait.

When South wins in dummy and leads a trump, East hops up with the ace, leads a heart for West to ruff, and receives a diamond ruff in return for the defenders' fourth trick.

BIDDING QUIZ

You hold: ♠ A 2 ♥ A Q 10 8 6 3 ♦ 4 ♣ Q 10 7 5. You open one heart, and your partner bids one spade. You rebid two hearts, he tries 2NT. The opponents pass. What do you say?

ANSWER: Bid three clubs, suggesting a minimum opening bid with six hearts and four clubs. (With most other heart-club distributions or with extra strength, you would bid clubs at your second turn.) Partner can pass or bid three or four hearts, but he must not insist on 3NT.

```
Dlr: South          ♠ K 10 8 3
Vul: N-S            ♥ 9 7 4
                    ♦ A K J 7 3
                    ♣ 8
♠ 7 6                               ♠ A 2
♥ 2                                 ♥ A Q 10 8 6 3
♦ 10 9 8 6 2                        ♦ 4
♣ J 9 6 3 2                         ♣ Q 10 7 5
                    ♠ Q J 9 5 4
                    ♥ K J 5
                    ♦ Q 5
                    ♣ A K 4
```

South	West	North	East
1♠	Pass	2♦	2♥
2 NT	Pass	4♠	All Pass

Opening lead: ♥2

55.

Expert Reasoning

Two-time world champion Eddie Kantar brought home the slam in the deal below. A lesser player might have done the same, but not for the best of reasons.

Kantar ruffed the opening lead and cashed the A-K of trumps. When East discarded, the contract depended on whether declarer could find the queen of diamonds. Biding his time, Kantar led a third trump to West's queen, ruffed the spade return, took the high clubs and ruffed dummy's last club. He then led the king and another diamond.

Fluff

Most players, for lack of anything better, would put up the ace of diamonds because of "eight ever, nine never". Experts hate to rely on such fluff. When Kantar played the ace to drop East's queen, he had a solid reason.

The vulnerability had beckoned East-West to compete in spades; yet, they hadn't uttered a peep. East had shown one heart and four clubs. With seven spades, would East have passed at every turn?

Kantar thought not. He placed East with only six spades — therefore, 6-1-2-4 distribution — and duly made the slam.

BIDDING QUIZ

You hold: ♠ K 10 9 8 6 ♥ Q 6 4 ♦ 10 6 ♣ 6 5 4. Your partner opens 2NT, and the next player passes. What do you say?

ANSWER: Bid three spades. If partner had opened 1NT, a bid of two spades would ask him to pass. Any response to 2NT, however, is forcing. Partner should return to 3NT with a doubleton spade, raise to four spades with three-card support, or bid a new suit with a maximum hand and an excellent spade fit.

```
Dlr: South        ♠ J 5
Vul: N-S          ♥ 9 8 3
                  ♦ A J 8 4
                  ♣ A Q 10 9
  ♠ K 10 9 8 6                    ♠ A Q 7 4 3 2
  ♥ Q 6 4                         ♥ J
  ♦ 10 6                          ♦ Q 9
  ♣ 6 5 4                         ♣ J 8 7 3
                  ♠ None
                  ♥ A K 10 7 5 2
                  ♦ K 7 5 3 2
                  ♣ K 2
```

South	West	North	East
1♥	Pass	2♣	Pass
2♦	Pass	3♥	Pass
4♦	Pass	5♣	Pass
6♥	All Pass		

Opening lead: ♠ 10

56.

Can't Take a Yolk?

South in the deal below adopted a poor line of play and wound up with egg on his face.

North's hand was well worth the slam try of five hearts. Thus egged on, South bid the slam. After South won the ace of clubs at the first trick, however, he trod on eggshells by leading a trump to the king and taking a finesse with the jack of trumps. This play laid an egg when West won the queen and the defense cashed a club to defeat the contract.

Discards Club

"You put all your eggs in one basket," North grumbled. "Cash the A-K of trumps. If the queen falls, you make the slam easily. If instead both opponents follow with low trumps, take the top three spades next and discard a club. When the jack falls, you throw your last club on the ten of spades.

"If the jack of spades doesn't fall, you're still safe if the defender with the queen of trumps has three or more diamonds."

"I get three chances instead of one," South noted.

"Eggs-actly," North said ruefully, "but you can't unscramble scrambled eggs."

True. And this write-up is ova.

BIDDING QUIZ

You hold: ♠ A Q 10 3 ♥ K 10 5 4 ♦ A Q 3 ♣ 9 2. Dealer, at your right, opens one diamond. You double, and your partner bids two spades. The opponents pass. What do you say?

ANSWER: Partner's jump response to your takeout double promises about 10 points. His bid is not forcing, but does invite game. Since your hand is worth 16 points, and any finesses your partner must try figure to work, bid four spades.

Dlr: South	♠ A Q 10 3	
Vul: N-S	♥ K 10 5 4	
	♦ A Q 3	
	♣ 9 2	

♠ 9 7 6 5		♠ J 8 2
♥ Q 8 2		♥ 9 7
♦ 5 4		♦ 10 9 7 6
♣ Q J 10 4		♣ K 8 6 5

	♠ K 4	
	♥ A J 6 3	
	♦ K J 8 2	
	♣ A 7 3	

South	West	North	East
1 NT	Pass	2♣	Pass
2♥	Pass	5♥	Pass
6♥	All Pass		

Opening lead: ♣Q

57.

Dlr: North
Vul: N-S

♠ Q 9 4
♥ A 5 3
♦ A Q 4
♣ Q 9 6 2

♠ K J 10 7 5 2
♥ K 8
♦ 10 6 3
♣ A 4

North	East	South	West
1♣	Pass	1♠	Pass
1 NT	Pass	4♠	All Pass

West leads the ♥Q. Plan the play. (Trumps are 2-2.)

58.

Dlr: South
Vul: Both

♠ A K 2
♥ A 7 6 5 4
♦ 5 4
♣ K 7 6

♠ J 10 9 8 7
♥ K 3
♦ A K J 2
♣ A 4

South	West	North	East
1♠	Pass	2♥	Pass
3♦	Pass	4♠	Pass
5♣	Pass	6♠	All Pass

West leads the ♣10. Plan the play.

FRANK STEWART

59.

Dlr: East
Vul: None

♠ A J 7 4
♥ 10 6 4
♦ J 5 3
♣ K 7 3

♠ Q 10 8 6 3 2
♥ K 5
♦ 9 6 4
♣ A 5

East	South	West	North
Pass	Pass	1♦	Pass
2♣	2♠	3♣	3♠
All Pass			

West cashes the ♦K and ♦A, and East drops the queen on the second lead. East ruffs the next diamond with the ♠9, cashes the ♥A and leads another heart. How do you play the trumps?

60.

Dlr: North
Vul: N-S

♠ A K 9 8
♥ 9 6 5 4
♦ K J
♣ 6 4 2

♠ J 10 6
♥ A K Q J 7 3 2
♦ None
♣ K 5 3

North	East	South	West
Pass	Pass	4♥	All Pass

West leads the ♥10. East follows. Plan the play.

57.

Act of Congress

Because of the deal below, a bridge-playing member of Congress has introduced the High-Card Practices Act. This act would require at least 26 points to undertake any game contract.

Congressman South took the first heart with the king, led a trump to West's ace, won the next heart and drew trumps. South then led a diamond to finesse with the queen. When East won the king and returned a diamond, declarer had four losers.

South noted that game was cold with one more point (say, the jack of clubs). The next day, he called in the Legislative Drafting Service.

Makes Game

Readers can save some tax dollars. When you next write your Congressman, mention that South can easily make his game with only his 25 points.

After South wins the ace of hearts, he must ruff a heart. He then draws trumps and leads the ace of clubs and a low club to dummy's nine.

When East wins the ten, he must give South the tenth trick with any lead. A heart, if East had one to lead, would yield a ruff-sluff; a diamond lead goes into the A-Q; and if East returns a club, South discards a diamond and wins a trick with the queen of clubs no matter who has the king.

BIDDING QUIZ

You hold: ♠ Q 9 4 ♥ A 5 3 ♦ A Q 4 ♣ Q 9 6 2. Your partner opens one heart, you respond 2NT, and he next bids three diamonds. The opponents pass. What do you say?

ANSWER: Bid three hearts. Partner is nervous about notrump and would love to know that you have three cards in his first suit. If your hearts were stronger, you could jump to four hearts, but to insist on 3NT would be a major breach of discipline.

```
Dlr: North          ♠ Q 9 4
Vul: N-S            ♥ A 5 3
                    ♦ A Q 4
                    ♣ Q 9 6 2
♠ A 3                               ♠ 8 6
♥ Q J 10 4 2                        ♥ 9 7 6
♦ J 9 8                             ♦ K 7 5 2
♣ J 7 3                             ♣ K 10 8 5
                    ♠ K J 10 7 5 2
                    ♥ K 8
                    ♦ 10 6 3
                    ♣ A 4
```

North	East	South	West
1♣	Pass	1♠	Pass
1 NT	Pass	4♠	All Pass

Opening lead: ♥Q

FRANK STEWART

58.

Easy When You See It

South saw that he could make the six-spade contract by ruffing two losers in dummy. He took the king of clubs, cashed the top diamonds and ruffed a diamond with the deuce of spades. That play ended the suspense early. East overruffed and got the queen of spades later to defeat the slam.

"Maybe I should try to set up hearts," declarer second-guessed himself.

"Maybe," East responded, "but that play won't work either. Hearts split four-two, and spades split four-one. If you ruff two hearts, you lose control."

"Well, what could I have done?" South sought enlightenment.

12 Tricks

"Ever hear the expression 'Never send a deuce to do an ace's job'?" East asked. "Ruff a diamond with the ace of trumps, come to the ace of clubs and ruff your last diamond with the king of trumps. Then lead the deuce of trumps. With decent breaks, you can draw trumps and take twelve tricks."

The line of play East suggested was simplest and best. Actually, South can get home in another way: ace of clubs, A-K of diamonds, K-A of hearts, heart ruff, trump to dummy's king, heart ruff, club to the king, club ruff, diamond ruff with the ace, heart. East can't stop South from scoring his last trump *en passant* for the 12th trick.

BIDDING QUIZ

You hold: ♠ A K 2 ♥ A 7 6 5 4 ♦ 5 4 ♣ K 7 6. You open one heart, and your partner responds 1NT. The opponents pass. What do you say?

ANSWER: Pass. 1NT should be as good a contract as any. To rebid the hearts would be a blunder, since partner might have to pass with a singleton or void in hearts. Although rebidding a five-card suit is permissible, a rebid of two hearts in this situation would promise at least a six-card suit.

```
Dlr: South          ♠ A K 2
Vul: Both           ♥ A 7 6 5 4
                    ♦ 5 4
                    ♣ K 7 6
 ♠ 4                                ♠ Q 6 5 3
 ♥ Q 10 9 8                         ♥ J 2
 ♦ Q 10 7 6 3                       ♦ 9 8
 ♣ 10 9 8                           ♣ Q J 5 3 2
                    ♠ J 10 9 8 7
                    ♥ K 3
                    ♦ A K J 2
                    ♣ A 4
```

South	West	North	East
1♠	Pass	2♥	Pass
3♦	Pass	4♠	Pass
5♣	Pass	6♠	All Pass

Opening lead: ♣10

59.

Infer, Don't Assume

An assumption is something you take for granted; an inference is backed up by evidence. Therefore, when you must locate a missing honor, a solid inference is a far more reliable guide.

West took the top diamonds, crashing East's queen, and led a third diamond. East ruffed, cashed the ace of hearts and led a heart to South's king.

Declarer then led the queen of trumps, hoping West would be foolish enough to cover. When West produced the five, South huddled and finally played low from dummy. Down one.

Distribution

"The opening bidder figured to have the king of trumps," South defended his play; but instead of making a hazy assumption about high-card points, South should try to infer the East-West distribution.

South knows that West had five diamonds to East's two. Each defender must have four hearts; otherwise, someone would surely have bid hearts. Finally, West needs at least three-card club support for his raise to three clubs.

Therefore, West's five of trumps must be a singleton, and South should put up dummy's ace to drop East's king.

BIDDING QUIZ

You hold: ♠ Q 10 8 6 3 2 ♥ K 5 ♦ 9 6 4 ♣ A 5. Your partner opens 1NT, and the next player passes. What do you say?

ANSWER: When your partner opens 1NT, you are responsible for placing the contract; he has described his hand. Here, your hand is worth about 12 points, more than enough to insist on game, and you know your side has at least eight spades for trumps. Don't shirk your duty; jump to four spades.

```
        Dlr: East          ♠ A J 7 4
        Vul: None          ♥ 10 6 4
                           ♦ J 5 3
                           ♣ K 7 3
    ♠ 5                                      ♠ K 9
    ♥ Q J 7 3                                ♥ A 9 8 2
    ♦ A K 10 7 2                             ♦ Q 8
    ♣ Q 9 2                                  ♣ J 10 8 6 4
                           ♠ Q 10 8 6 3 2
                           ♥ K 5
                           ♦ 9 6 4
                           ♣ A 5
```

East	South	West	North
Pass	Pass	1♦	Pass
2♣	2♠	3♣	3♠
All Pass			

Opening lead: ♦K

FRANK STEWART

60.

A Colorful Deal

South won the opening trump lead and promptly led the jack of spades for a finesse. When East took the queen and led the queen of clubs, South went white as a sheet, while West was pink with pleasure. The defense got three club tricks to maroon South with a minus score and put him in a black mood.

North turned purple; he favored South with a few blue remarks about his dummy play.

"A winning spade finesse gives me an overtrick," South argued. "If I don't try it, you'll think I'm yellow."

Gray Hairs

South was obviously a green declarer. He can spare himself a red face (and some gray hairs) if he sets up a trick in spades while keeping East off lead. South must go to dummy at the second trick, lead the king of diamonds and throw a spade if East plays low. South later takes the A-K of spades and leads the nine for a ruffing finesse, setting up his tenth trick wherever the queen of spades lies.

If East were to cover the king of diamonds with the ace, South would ruff, return to dummy and lead the jack of diamonds with the same plan in mind.

BIDDING QUIZ

You hold: ♠ 5 4 3 ♥ 10 ♦ A 9 8 6 4 ♣ A 10 8 7. Your partner opens one heart, you respond 1NT, and he rebids three hearts. The opponents pass. What do you say?

ANSWER: Since partner promises about 17 points, game is likely. Your aces are valuable cards, and the ten of hearts is adequate support — as good as two low cards — when partner promises a suit of six good hearts. Bid four hearts.

```
Dlr: North          ♠ A K 9 8
Vul: N-S            ♥ 9 6 5 4
                    ♦ K J
                    ♣ 6 4 2
  ♠ 5 4 3                          ♠ Q 7 2
  ♥ 10                             ♥ 8
  ♦ A 9 8 6 4                      ♦ Q 10 7 5 3 2
  ♣ A 10 8 7                       ♣ Q J 9
                    ♠ J 10 6
                    ♥ A K Q J 7 3 2
                    ♦ None
                    ♣ K 5 3
```

North	East	South	West
Pass	Pass	4♥	All Pass

Opening lead: ♥10

61.

Dlr: West
Vul: E-W

♠ K J 6 3
♥ Q 7 5
♦ A 10 3
♣ 9 5 3

```
      N
   W     E
      S
```

♠ Q 10 4
♥ 10 6
♦ 9 6 4 2
♣ A K Q 4

West	North	East	South
Pass	Pass	Pass	1 NT
Pass	2♣	Pass	2♠
Pass	4♠	All Pass	

West leads the ♣2. Plan the defense.

62.

Dlr: South
Vul: N-S

♠ Q 4 2
♥ J 10 9
♦ 9 5
♣ K Q J 9 4

♠ A 7 6 5
♥ A K 4 3
♦ A K 3
♣ 10 3

South	West	North	East
1 NT	Pass	3 NT	All Pass

West leads the ♥2. Plan the play.

63.

Dlr: South		♠ K 9 5	
Vul: Both		♥ K J 10 8 5	
		♦ A J 3	
		♣ 7 3	

```
        ┌─────┐      ♠ 7 3
        │  N  │      ♥ 9 7 4
        │W   E│      ♦ K 10 2
        │  S  │      ♣ A 9 8 5 4
        └─────┘
```

South	West	North	East
1♠	Pass	2♥	Pass
2♠	Pass	4♠	All Pass

West leads the ♣Q. Plan the defense.

64.

Dlr: South		♠ A 5 4	
Vul: E-W		♥ K Q 4 3	
		♦ A J	
		♣ 10 6 5 2	

```
              ♠ Q
              ♥ 9
              ♦ Q 9 7 6 5 4 3 2
              ♣ 9 7 4
```

South	West	North	East
4♦	Pass	5♦	All Pass

West leads the ♠3. Do you see any way out of this mess?

61.

Hide And Seek

A bridge deal may contain a game within a game. While declarer is busy reconstructing the missing hands, the defenders try to keep their holdings concealed. It's a game of hide and seek.

In the deal below, an average East wins with the queen of clubs at the first trick, the lowest of his equals, and continues with the king and ace. South ruffs and tries a finesse with dummy's jack of spades, losing to East's queen. South wins the heart return, draws trumps and can claim his game. Since East, who didn't open the bidding, has produced 11 high-card points, West is sure to hold the queen of diamonds.

No Cakewalk

In an expert game, South has no such cakewalk. East takes the first trick with the ace of clubs and leads the queen. When South's jack falls, East next leads a low club, concealing the king!

South is then sure that West has the king of clubs, and from South's point of view, either defender may hold the queen of diamonds. South may still guess right in diamonds, but his contract hasn't been handed to him on a platter.

Hide and seek: a children's game, but an exquisite aspect of bridge.

BIDDING QUIZ

You hold: ♠ Q 10 4 ♥ 10 6 ♦ 9 6 4 2 ♣ A K Q 4. Your partner deals and opens 2NT. The next player passes. What do you say?

ANSWER: Bid 6NT. With 11 high-card points and two tens, you are entitled to bid slam even if partner can have as few as 21 points for his opening bid. It's a long leap to the six level, but you must view this situation as an opportunity to grasp. It's up to you to place the contract, so do your duty.

```
Dlr: West          ♠ K J 6 3
Vul: E-W           ♥ Q 7 5
                   ♦ A 10 3
                   ♣ 9 5 3

♠ 8 2                              ♠ Q 10 4
♥ J 9 8 3                          ♥ 10 6
♦ Q 8 7                            ♦ 9 6 4 2
♣ 10 7 6 2                         ♣ A K Q 4

                   ♠ A 9 7 5
                   ♥ A K 4 2
                   ♦ K J 5
                   ♣ J 8
```

West	North	East	South
Pass	Pass	Pass	1 NT
Pass	2♣	Pass	2♠
Pass	4♠	All Pass	

Opening lead: ♣2

62.

Free Spirit

My friend Freda Freeman fights the good fight with life by ferreting out freebies. 'If it's free, I want it' is her creed. Her achievements range from dinners to plane tickets — all gratis.

At the bridge table, Freda champions free bids and free raises, indulges in free doubles when the opponents have a leg, and has a particular passion for 100 honors. ("They're just like a free gift," she says, using a favorite, if redundant, term.)

Freda, South in the deal below, cackled at West's opening heart lead. Elated by getting a free finesse, she won the first heart with dummy's jack.

Second Club

Alas, when Freda attacked clubs, East took the second club and led a heart. Freda won the ace and tried to reach dummy with the queen of spades. When East produced the king, my penny-wise friend finished with only seven tricks.

Freda makes her game by paying a fair price to win the first trick: the king of hearts. If East then leads a diamond after taking the ace of clubs, declarer wins and leads a low heart. West can't stop Freda from winning a heart trick in dummy and enjoying the clubs.

BIDDING QUIZ

You hold: ♠ K J 9 3 ♥ 7 6 ♦ Q 10 7 4 ♣ A 5 2. Dealer, at your left, opens one club, and your partner doubles. You bid two spades, and partner raises to three spades. What do you say?

ANSWER: Your jump invited game and promised at least nine points. Partner's raise promised a little more than an opening bid. Since all your points will be useful, and the ace of clubs is a good card opposite partner's probable shortness, bid four spades.

```
Dlr: South          ♠ Q 4 2
Vul: N-S            ♥ J 10 9
                    ♦ 9 5
                    ♣ K Q J 9 4
♠ 10 8                              ♠ K J 9 3
♥ Q 8 5 2                           ♥ 7 6
♦ J 8 6 2                           ♦ Q 10 7 4
♣ 8 7 6                             ♣ A 5 2
                    ♠ A 7 6 5
                    ♥ A K 4 3
                    ♦ A K 3
                    ♣ 10 3
```

South	West	North	East
1 NT	Pass	3 NT	All Pass

Opening lead: ♥2

63.

Defense Wooden Work

An expression bridge writers love to use in castigating bad defense is, "East woodenly returned a spade". This phrase has appeared in print so often that I'd use it only if East were John Wooden, the famous UCLA basketball coach.

East in the deal below took the ace of clubs at the first trick, pined over his return and, wooden you know it, led back a club. South won, drew trumps and forced out the ace of hearts.

West's face was ashen. "Fir cryin' out loud," he moaned at East as he switched to a diamond. "Didn't you cedar strong hearts in dummy?" South took the ace of diamonds and finished with an overtrick.

Diamond Shift

East, who obviously couldn't see the forest for the trees, must shift to a low diamond at the second trick. West needs either a spade or heart trick for the defenders to have a chance. Even so, the defenders also need two diamond tricks to defeat the game, and they must establish them quickly, before South draws trumps and sets up dummy's hearts for discards.

Oaks may grow from acorns, but good defense is based on simple ideas.

BIDDING QUIZ

You hold: ♠ 8 2 ♥ A 3 2 ♦ Q 8 6 5 ♣ Q J 10 2. Your partner opens one club, you raise to two clubs, and he rebids 2NT. The opponents pass. What do you say?

ANSWER: Your partner must be interested in game, else he would pass two clubs (no matter what sort of flimsy suit he may have opened on). Since you could hardly have a better hand for your single raise, you should accept his invitation. Bid 3NT.

```
Dlr: South          ♠ K 9 5
Vul: Both           ♥ K J 10 8 5
                    ♦ A J 3
                    ♣ 7 3
♠ 8 2                               ♠ 7 3
♥ A 3 2                             ♥ 9 7 4
♦ Q 8 6 5                           ♦ K 10 2
♣ Q J 10 2                          ♣ A 9 8 5 4
                    ♠ A Q J 10 6 4
                    ♥ Q 6
                    ♦ 9 7 4
                    ♣ K 6
```

South	West	North	East
1♠	Pass	2♥	Pass
2♠	Pass	4♠	All Pass

Opening lead: ♣Q

64.

The Perils of Goldman

Some deals resemble an old-time movie serial, with the hero in constant peril, but always managing to escape the villain's clutches. The hero on the deal below, which arose in a major team championship, was expert Bobby Goldman.

Goldman's preempt was hardly classical, but North's raise was no thing of beauty either. In any case, the contract could safely be called perilous.

West could have defeated Goldman three tricks with a heart or club opening lead, but it wasn't his day; he tried a spade. Goldman saw only a ghostly chance of survival. Desperately, he played low from dummy and won his singleton queen.

Ruffing Finesse

Next, declarer led a trump to finesse with the jack. He threw his heart on the ace of spades and led the king of hearts for a ruffing finesse. Lady Luck was still there; East covered with the ace of hearts. Goldman ruffed, got to dummy with a trump and pitched a club on the queen of hearts. He lost only two clubs.

I don't know if East and West snarled, "Curses, foiled again," but I wouldn't blame them if they did.

BIDDING QUIZ

You hold: ♠ J 10 9 7 ♥ A 8 5 2 ♦ 8 ♣ K Q J 3. Dealer, at your right, opens one diamond, and you double. Partner responds two clubs. The opponents pass. What do you say?

ANSWER: Pass. Don't be seduced by your magnificent clubs. Partner made a minimum response, indicating fewer than nine points, and even eight tricks may be hard to take. If partner responds cheaply to your takeout double, you need substantial extra strength to bid again.

```
Dlr: South        ♠ A 5 4
Vul: E-W          ♥ K Q 4 3
                  ♦ A J
                  ♣ 10 6 5 2

♠ K 8 6 3 2                       ♠ J 10 9 7
♥ J 10 7 6                        ♥ A 8 5 2
♦ K 10                            ♦ 8
♣ A 8                             ♣ K Q J 3

                  ♠ Q
                  ♥ 9
                  ♦ Q 9 7 6 5 4 3 2
                  ♣ 9 7 4
```

South	West	North	East
4♦	Pass	5♦	All Pass

Opening lead: ♠3

65.

Dlr: South
Vul: E-W

♠ A Q J
♥ None
♦ A 8 6 3 2
♣ Q J 4 3 2

♠ K 10 9 8
♥ J 8 6 4
♦ K 4
♣ A K 5

South	West	North	East
1♣	Pass	1♦	Pass
1♥	Pass	3♣	Pass
3♠	Pass	6♣	All Pass

West leads the ♦10. East follows low. Plan the play.

66.

Dlr: South
Vul: N-S

♠ 6 4
♥ 6 5 3
♦ K J 10 7 6 3
♣ A J

```
      N
   W     E
      S
```

♠ Q 10 3
♥ A 10
♦ A Q 4
♣ 9 6 5 4 2

South	West	North	East
1 NT	Pass	3 NT	All Pass

West leads the ♥4. Plan the defense.

67.

Dlr: South
Vul: None

♠ 7 6
♥ A 6
♦ A Q 10 6 5
♣ K J 7 2

```
      N
   W     E
      S
```

♠ A K 8 5 2
♥ K 3
♦ 9 7
♣ Q 10 4 3

South	West	North	East
3♥	Pass	4♥	All Pass

West leads the ♠Q and continues with the ♠J. How should
East defend?

68.

Dlr: West
Vul: None

♠ A 9 2
♥ K J 3
♦ 8 5
♣ 9 6 4 3 2

♠ J 6
♥ A 9 8 6 4 2
♦ 10 3
♣ A K J

West	North	East	South
Pass	Pass	Pass	1♥
Pass	2♥	Dbl	3♥
Pass	4♥	All Pass	

West leads the ♦2. East cashes the king and ace and shifts to
a low spade: jack, king. Plan the play.

65.

Of Boys and Men

South took his king of diamonds at the first trick and returned a diamond toward dummy. When West correctly refused to ruff a loser, South won dummy's ace and led a third diamond.

"Never send a boy to do a man's job," declarer murmured as he ruffed with the king of clubs. He next got to dummy with a spade and put another elder of the tribe — the ace of clubs — to the task of ruffing a fourth diamond.

South then ruffed a heart in dummy and cashed the Q-J of trumps. When trumps unkindly broke 4-1, he lost two trump tricks and his slam.

Child Labor

On this occasion, South can stoop to using child labor. He must ruff the third diamond with the puerile five of trumps.

If West discards, South has 12 easy tricks. Even if West overruffs, South is safe. South ruffs the heart return in dummy and can afford to ruff a fourth diamond with the manly ace of trumps. South still wins 12 tricks: five trumps in dummy, two high diamonds, one diamond ruff in his hand and four spades.

BIDDING QUIZ

You hold: ♠ K 10 9 8 ♥ J 8 6 4 ♦ K 4 ♣ A K 5. Your partner opens one club, you respond one heart, and he raises to two hearts. The opponents pass. What do you say?

ANSWER: You should have a game, but you may not belong at hearts even though partner has raised. (He may have only three-card support.) Bid two spades. Partner will insist on hearts if he has four good trumps and unbalanced distribution. If he next bids 2NT, though, raise to 3NT.

```
Dlr: South          ♠ A Q J
Vul: E-W            ♥ None
                    ♦ A 8 6 3 2
                    ♣ Q J 4 3 2
♠ 7 5 4 2                           ♠ 6 3
♥ K 10 7 3                          ♥ A Q 9 5 2
♦ 10                                ♦ Q J 9 7 5
♣ 10 8 7 6                          ♣ 9
                    ♠ K 10 9 8
                    ♥ J 8 6 4
                    ♦ K 4
                    ♣ A K 5
```

South	West	North	East
1♣	Pass	1♦	Pass
1♥	Pass	3♣	Pass
3♠	Pass	6♣	All Pass

Opening lead: ♦ 10

66.

Rules Can Be Broken

Once upon a time, when bridge was played strictly by rules, you always returned your partner's lead. (The only excuse for shifting was having no card in his suit, and even then partner would feel entitled to grumble at you a bit.) Nowadays, good players pay scant attention to such notions.

East in the deal below took the ace of hearts and, still living in the past, returned the ten of hearts. This play let South make his contract. He won the king and led the nine of diamonds for a finesse. East played low, took the next diamond with the queen and led a spade. South won the ace, lost to the ace of diamonds and ended up with ten tricks.

Attacks Entry

East should forget the idea of returning partner's lead. Since on the bidding West can hold at most three points, the heart suit cannot be a source of defensive tricks.

East defeats the contract by switching to a club at the second trick, threatening dummy's entries. When East wins the second diamond with the queen, he leads a second club. The diamond suit is now dead, and South can win only one diamond trick, two spades, two hearts and three clubs.

BIDDING QUIZ

You hold: ♠ Q 10 3 ♥ A 10 ♦ A Q 4 ♣ 9 6 5 4 2. Your partner opens one club, and the next player passes. What do you say?

ANSWER: Bid 2NT. Though you have club support, you should aim for the cheaper notrump game. 2NT describes your hand well: you have 13 points, balanced distribution and tricks in the unbid suits. If partner has unbalanced pattern, he has plenty of room to try for an alternate contract.

```
Dlr: South          ♠ 6 4
Vul: N-S            ♥ 6 5 3
                   ♦ K J 10 7 6 3
                   ♣ A J
♠ J 9 8 5                        ♠ Q 10 3
♥ J 8 7 4 2                      ♥ A 10
♦ 2                              ♦ A Q 4
♣ 8 7 3                          ♣ 9 6 5 4 2
                   ♠ A K 7 2
                   ♥ K Q 9
                   ♦ 9 8 5
                   ♣ K Q 10
```

South	West	North	East
1 NT	Pass	3 NT	All Pass

Opening lead: ♥4

67.

Protect Your Partner

When bridge players discuss deals, a favorite pastime is assessing the blame for defensive disasters. Decide who presented South with his contract on the deal below.

After winning the first trick, West continued with the jack of spades. Everyone followed low, and West next led a low club. South rose with dummy's king, cashed the ace of hearts, ruffed a club and ruffed his last spade in dummy. He ruffed another club, lost a trick to the king of trumps and claimed his game.

Overtakes

The defensive postmortem was brief and to the point. East said that West's club underlead was the worst play in bridge history, and West said that East didn't realize he had a partner at the table. Whom do you believe?

I assign the blame to East. West had no way to know that East had a trump trick. From West's vantage point, the only chance to defeat the contract might have been to put South to an early guess in clubs.

East, however, knew that the contract was down if West had the ace of clubs. East should overtake the second spade with the king and return a club, protecting his partner from making an error.

BIDDING QUIZ

You hold: ♠ A K 8 5 2 ♥ K 3 ♦ 9 7 ♣ Q 10 4 3. You open one spade, and your partner responds 1NT. The opponents pass. What do you say?

ANSWER: Bid two clubs. Since your pattern is unbalanced, try again for a suit contract. Partner can pass, raise clubs, return to spades or bid two of a red suit (which you will pass). You must not rebid two spades; if partner had one spade and four clubs, you'd be to blame for reaching a terrible contract.

```
Dlr: South        ♠ 7 6
Vul: None         ♥ A 6
                  ♦ A Q 10 6 5
                  ♣ K J 7 2
♠ Q J 9                         ♠ A K 8 5 2
♥ 9 7                           ♥ K 3
♦ J 8 3 2                       ♦ 9 7
♣ A 9 8 5                       ♣ Q 10 4 3
                  ♠ 10 4 3
                  ♥ Q J 10 8 5 4 2
                  ♦ K 4
                  ♣ 6
```

South	West	North	East
3♥	Pass	4♥	All Pass

Opening lead: ♠Q

68.

Eights and Nines

North's bid of four hearts was wrong, since South would have re-doubled two hearts if he were interested in game; the actual bid of three hearts was intended as a preempt. Unfortunately, South's dummy play matched his partner's bidding.

After taking two high diamonds, East led a spade, and West covered South's jack with the king. South won dummy's ace and cashed the A-K of hearts.

When East threw a spade, declarer muttered something about "eight ever, nine never." Undaunted, he next led a club to finesse with the jack. West produced the queen, took his high trump and led a spade to East's queen. Down two.

Rhymes

South relied too much on nursery rhymes. East must hold A-K-J in diamonds; if West held Q-J-x-x, he would lead the queen. East is also marked with a high spade, since West would prefer a spade lead from K-Q-x-x to a diamond from Q-x-x-x.

Thus, West must have the queen of hearts and queen of clubs. If East had either card, he would have opened the bidding.

South should therefore lead a heart to the ace and return a heart to finesse with dummy's jack. After drawing trumps, he takes the A-K of clubs. When the queen falls from West, South loses only two diamonds and a spade.

BIDDING QUIZ

You hold: ♠ J 6 ♥ A 9 8 6 4 2 ♦ 10 3 ♣ A K J. You open one heart, and your partner responds one spade. You rebid two hearts, he tries three diamonds. The opponents pass. What do you say?

ANSWER: You need not bid hearts a third time; the rebid of two hearts promised at least a six-card suit. (If you held only five hearts, you could have bid a new suit, raised spades or bid 1NT over partner's one-spade response.) Bid 3NT.

Dlr: West	♠ A 9 2		
Vul: None	♥ K J 3		
	♦ 8 5		
	♣ 9 6 4 3 2		

♠ K 8 5 3		♠ Q 10 7 4
♥ Q 10 5		♥ 7
♦ Q 9 4 2		♦ A K J 7 6
♣ Q 7		♣ 10 8 5

	♠ J 6
	♥ A 9 8 6 4 2
	♦ 10 3
	♣ A K J

West	North	East	South
Pass	Pass	Pass	1♥
Pass	2♥	Dbl	3♥
Pass	4♥	All Pass	

Opening lead: ♦2

69.

Dlr: South		♠ K 10 9 7	
Vul: N-S		♥ 8 3	
		♦ 7 5 4 2	
		♣ A J 10	

		♠ A Q J 8 6 4 2	
		♥ A Q	
		♦ A Q 6 3	
		♣ None	

South	West	North	East
1♠	2♣	2♠	Pass
3♦	Pass	4♠	Pass
6♠	All Pass		

West leads the ♣K. Plan the play.

70.

Dlr: North		♠ Q 10 9	
Vul: None		♥ K 5 3	
		♦ K 7 2	
		♣ 8 6 4 3	

		♠ A J 2	
		♥ A J 9 8 6 2	
		♦ 8 3	
		♣ A Q	

North	East	South	West
Pass	Pass	1♥	Pass
2♥	Dbl	4♥	All Pass

West leads the ♦Q and ♦J. You ruff East's ace on the third
diamond lead. How do you continue?

71.

Dlr: South
Vul: N-S

♠ None
♥ A 7 4 2
♦ 5 3
♣ A J 9 6 5 4 2

♠ A Q 5
♥ J 6
♦ K Q J 10 6 4
♣ Q 8

South	West	North	East
1♦	2♣	3♣	3♠
3 NT	All Pass		

West leads the ♠8, and you win the queen. Perhaps you wouldn't have passed 3NT with North's card, but how do you continue to make the contract?

72.

Dlr: South
Vul: N-S

♠ A K 6 5 4
♥ Q 9 3
♦ A K J
♣ J 3

```
      N
   W     E
      S
```

♠ J 8 2
♥ K J 10 7 2
♦ Q 10 8
♣ A 2

South	West	North	East
3♣	Pass	3♠	Pass
3 NT	All Pass		

West leads the ♥8. Dummy covers with the nine, you play the ten, and South follows with the four. How do you continue?

69.

Find the 12th Trick

The winning play in the deal below is hard to see even with 52 cards in view. Can you spot it?

The actual South gave the slam a feeble try. After throwing the queen of hearts on the ace of clubs, he finessed with the queen of diamonds. When West took the king, declarer was sunk; eventually, he lost another diamond and went down.

After the opening lead, South has seven trump tricks and three side aces, plus a second club trick available with the J-10. To find a 12th trick, he should look to diamonds.

Discards

South pitches a diamond on the ace of clubs at the first trick and another on the jack of clubs at the second trick. Suppose West takes the queen and leads a trump. South wins in his hand, cashes the ace of diamonds, gets to dummy with a trump and throws the queen of diamonds on the ten of clubs.

South then ruffs a diamond, gets back to dummy with a trump and ruffs a diamond. He can then return with a trump and take dummy's last diamond to discard the queen of hearts.

Did you foresee that South would get home by setting up a long card in dummy?

BIDDING QUIZ

You hold: ♠ 3 ♥ J 9 7 6 4 2 ♦ 10 8 ♣ 8 6 4 3. Your partner deals and opens one heart, and the next player doubles. What do you say?

ANSWER: Some players would put their faith in a hoary tactic such as a psychic response of one spade, but such bluffs won't work against good opponents. The best strategy is to preempt as high as you dare. Unless the vulnerability is unfavorable, jump to four hearts.

```
Dlr: South          ♠ K 10 9 7
Vul: N-S            ♥ 8 3
                    ♦ 7 5 4 2
                    ♣ A J 10
♠ 5                                     ♠ 3
♥ K 10 5                                ♥ J 9 7 6 4 2
♦ K J 9                                 ♦ 10 8
♣ K Q 9 7 5 2                           ♣ 8 6 4 3
                    ♠ A Q J 8 6 4 2
                    ♥ A Q
                    ♦ A Q 6 3
                    ♣ None
```

South	West	North	East
1♠	2♣	2♠	Pass
3♦	Pass	4♠	Pass
6♠	All Pass		

Opening lead: ♣K

FRANK STEWART

70.

Second Opinion

"You're way overweight," pronounced the doctor after examining his patient.

"I want a second opinion," his charge demanded.

"Okay," the doc obliged. "You're ugly."

North in the deal below was an M.D, who possessed scarcely more tact. South ruffed the third diamond and cashed the A-K of trumps. When East threw a club, South needed winning finesses in both spades and clubs to make game.

Declarer first led dummy's ten of spades. Everyone followed low. When South led the queen of spades next, however, East covered with the king. Since South couldn't get back to dummy to finesse in clubs, he went down.

Diagnosis

"You misbid," North diagnosed. "When my raise to two hearts is doubled, you should redouble. When they run, you can bid three hearts to try for game and let me decide."

"I want a second opinion," South said skeptically.

"You misplayed too," was the response. "When you're in dummy, lead the queen of spades. If it isn't covered, drop the jack from your hand. Then lead the ten of spades. Whether or not East covers, you'll be able to try the club finesse."

BIDDING QUIZ

You hold: ♠ K 7 5 3 ♥ 7 ♦ A 10 6 5 ♣ K J 9 2. Your partner opens one heart, you respond one spade, he rebids two hearts, and you try 2NT. Partner next bids three diamonds. The opponents pass. What do you say?

ANSWER: Partner has six hearts, four diamonds and a minimum opening. With extra strength, he would bid diamonds at his second turn instead of limiting his hand with a rebid of two hearts. Three diamonds should have a chance, but not 3NT. Pass.

```
Dlr: North          ♠ Q 10 9
Vul: None           ♥ K 5 3
                    ♦ K 7 2
                    ♣ 8 6 4 3
♠ 8 6 4                             ♠ K 7 5 3
♥ Q 10 4                            ♥ 7
♦ Q J 9 4                           ♦ A 10 6 5
♣ 10 7 5                            ♣ K J 9 2
                    ♠ A J 2
                    ♥ A J 9 8 6 2
                    ♦ 8 3
                    ♣ A Q
```

North	East	South	West
Pass	Pass	1♥	Pass
2♥	Dbl	4♥	All Pass

Opening lead: ♦ Q

71.

Shakespeare Festival

It was the twelfth night of a big tournament, and South, a Venetian merchant, was playing against two gentlemen of Verona. After reaching an unlikely 3NT contract, South won the first trick with the queen of spades and led the queen of clubs for a finesse.

East played low, and South led another club. West discarded a diamond, and declarer put in dummy's jack and saw East's king "lear" at him. Still, all's well that ends well: East erred by returning a spade, and South won the ace, led to the ace of hearts and ran the clubs for nine tricks.

Spade Lead

The postmortem was a tempest. "What a comedy of errors," North exclaimed. "That spade opening lead ruined the defense."

West, however, gave back measure for measure. "Much ado about nothing," he retorted. "The contract still goes down if my partner returns the king of hearts instead of a spade at the fourth trick."

"As you like it," East acknowledged. "Yet, declarer could always have made his game."

After the queen of clubs wins at the second trick, South must lead a high diamond. If West takes the ace, South can get five diamond tricks, two spades, two clubs and the ace of hearts. If West refuses the first diamond, South shifts back to clubs for nine sure tricks.

BIDDING QUIZ

You hold: ♠ A Q 5 ♥ J 6 ♦ K Q J 10 6 4 ♣ Q 8. Your partner opens three clubs, and the next player passes. What do you say?

ANSWER: Pass. A bid of three diamonds would be strong and forcing and would promise game interest. (You have no reason to "correct" to three diamonds with a weak hand, since partner's clubs will make a good trump suit.) Second choice: a bid of four clubs to make it tough for the opponents to bid hearts.

```
Dlr: South          ♠ None
Vul: N-S            ♥ A 7 4 2
                    ♦ 5 3
                    ♣ A J 9 6 5 4 2
♠ K J 9 8 4 2                      ♠ 10 7 6 3
♥ 8 5 3                            ♥ K Q 10 9
♦ A 9 7                           ♦ 8 2
♣ 7                              ♣ K 10 3
                    ♠ A Q 5
                    ♥ J 6
                    ♦ K Q J 10 6 4
                    ♣ Q 8
```

South	West	North	East
1♦	2♠	3♣	3♠
3 NT	All Pass		

Opening lead: ♠8

72.

Fun-Seeker Finds Coup

East in the deal below was a jovial player whose creed was "Eat, drink and make merry." He managed to do all three when the deal appeared in a recent tournament.

Arriving late for the game, East barely had time to grab a hot dog and a soft drink before rushing to the table. He picked up his cards, wolfed down his lunch, heard the opponents bid game and saw West lead a high heart.

South covered with dummy's nine and played low when our hero produced the ten. Since South clearly had the ace of hearts, a heart return, East knew, would cost a trick. What to do?

Kills Entry

The Merrimac Coup is the lead of an honor to dislodge one of declarer's entries. (In 1898 an American coalship, the *Merrimac*, was scuttled in a Cuban harbor channel to maroon the Spanish fleet in port.) Having read his history, East executed the Merrimac Coup by leading the king of hearts at the second trick, and South's entry to his club suit vanished.

When East refused to take the ace on the first club lead, eight tricks was the best poor South could do. South had to stand by and watch East make merry — with his Merrimac.

BIDDING QUIZ

You hold: ♠ J 8 2 ♥ K J 10 7 2 ♦ Q 10 8 ♣ A 2. Your partner deals and opens 1NT, and the next player passes. What do you say?

ANSWER: Bid two clubs, Stayman. If your partner next bids two hearts, raise to game. If he rebids two diamonds or two spades, try 3NT. Since you have balanced distribution and honors in every suit, this is not the time to seek a 5-3 heart fit.

Dlr: South	♠ A K 6 5 4	
Vul: N-S	♥ Q 9 3	
	♦ A K J	
	♣ J 3	
♠ Q 10 9 3		♠ J 8 2
♥ 8 6		♥ K J 10 7 2
♦ 9 7 6 3 2		♦ Q 10 8
♣ 8 6		♣ A 2
	♠ 7	
	♥ A 5 4	
	♦ 5 4	
	♣ K Q 10 9 7 5 4	

South	West	North	East
3♣	Pass	3♠	Pass
3 NT	All Pass		

Opening lead: ♥8

73.

Dlr: South   ♠ A K J 6 4
Vul: N-S   ♥ 8 5 2
                ♦ J 9 4
                ♣ Q 6

                ♠ 2
                ♥ A Q 10 7 4 3
                ♦ Q 10 3
                ♣ A 8 3

South	West	North	East
1♥	Pass	1♠	Pass
2♥	Pass	3♥	Pass
4♥	All Pass		

West leads the ♣5, and dummy's queen is greeted by East's king. How do you play?

74.

Dlr: North   ♠ K J 10 9 5 2
Vul: N-S   ♥ K 6
                ♦ 10 4 2
                ♣ A Q

                ♠ Q
                ♥ None
                ♦ A Q 9 6 3
                ♣ K J 10 9 7 4 2

North	East	South	West
1♠	4♥	5♣	All Pass

West leads the ♥J. You cover with dummy's king and ruff East's ace. Plan the play.

75.

Dlr: North   ♠ A K 9 6
Vul: N-S   ♥ A K 3
               ♦ 6 5
               ♣ J 10 8 3

                           ♠ 5 2
           N   ♥ J 7
       W   E   ♦ A Q J 4 2
           S   ♣ 6 5 4 2

North	East	South	West
1♣	1♦	1♠	2♦
2♠	Pass	3♠	Pass
4♠	All Pass		

West leads the ♦9, and declarer drops the ten under your ace. Plan the defense.

76.

Dlr: North   ♠ A 7 5 2
Vul: None   ♥ K J 4
               ♦ A J 7 4 2
               ♣ J

               ♠ K J 9 4 3
               ♥ 10 5
               ♦ K 10 5 3
               ♣ K 4

North	East	South	West
1♦	Dbl	1♠	Pass
3♠	Pass	4♠	All Pass

West leads the ♥9. East takes the queen and ace, cashes the ace of clubs, and leads a third heart, won by dummy's king. How do you continue?

73.

Simple Rule

Once, in New York City, there lived a player who was prone to make sweeping pronouncements at the table.

"Never bid six unless it makes," he would intone after a slam had failed. His fellow players listened in amusement to his authoritative statements and took to calling him The Rabbi. His favorite dictum — "When the king is singleton, play the ace" — became known as The Rabbi's Rule.

In the deal below, South played dummy's queen of clubs at the first trick and took East's king with the ace. Since losers were all too plentiful, declarer risked an immediate finesse with the jack of spades.

Disaster

Disaster ensued when East won the queen. The defense took a club and two diamonds and later got two trump tricks when declarer misguessed in that suit as well. Down three!

South makes his game if he follows The Rabbi's Rule. Once he decides to finesse in spades, he should first cash the ace of hearts. When West's king falls, declarer takes the A-K of spades to throw a club, draws trumps with a finesse of the ten, and holds his losers to two diamonds and a club.

BIDDING QUIZ

You hold: ♠ Q 10 7 5 ♥ J 9 6 ♦ K 8 7 ♣ K 10 4. Dealer, at your left, opens one heart, and your partner doubles. You bid two spades, and partner raises to three spades. The opponents pass. What do you say?

ANSWER: Your jump response invited game and promised at least nine points. Since one of your points, the jack of hearts, is probably worthless, and your distribution is as flat as a pancake, pass.

```
Dlr: South          ♠ A K J 6 4
Vul: N-S            ♥ 8 5 2
                    ♦ J 9 4
                    ♣ Q 6
   ♠ 9 8 3                          ♠ Q 10 7 5
   ♥ K                              ♥ J 9 6
   ♦ A 6 5 2                        ♦ K 8 7
   ♣ J 9 7 5 2                      ♣ K 10 4
                    ♠ 2
                    ♥ A Q 10 7 4 3
                    ♦ Q 10 3
                    ♣ A 8 3
```

South	West	North	East
1♥	Pass	1♠	Pass
2♥	Pass	3♥	Pass
4♥	All Pass		

Opening lead: ♣5

FRANK STEWART

74.

Restraint Unrewarded

South ruffed the first heart and correctly led the queen of spades at the second trick. West took the ace and led another heart for South to ruff.

Declarer then tried to draw trumps with dummy's A-Q. When East discarded, South pitched two diamonds on the high spades and then led a diamond to finesse with the queen. West won the king and got out with a heart, leaving declarer with a diamond loser. Down one.

"Do you know," South sighed, "I almost jumped to six clubs with my hand? It's cold if trumps split evenly."

"You judged well to stay out of slam," North nodded, hiding his chagrin at losing an easy game and rubber.

Runs Spades

After ruffing the second heart, South gets to dummy with the ace of clubs and starts to run the spades. Two trumps remain undrawn at that point. After West ruffs the fourth spade, South can win any return, draw the last trump with the queen and finish the spades.

South loses an overtrick if trumps split 2-2; he safeguards the contract against the far more likely 3-1 split.

BIDDING QUIZ

You hold: ♠ K J 10 9 5 2 ♥ K 6 ♦ 10 4 2 ♣ A Q. Your partner opens one heart, you respond one spade, and he next bids two diamonds. The opponents pass. What do you say?

ANSWER: Bid three spades if partner won't pass. (Many pairs treat this jump as only invitational.) Otherwise, you must bid game yourself. Since spades will make an acceptable trump suit even if your partner has a low singleton, try four spades. 3NT is a close second choice.

```
Dlr: North          ♠ K J 10 9 5 2
Vul: N-S            ♥ K 6
                    ♦ 10 4 2
                    ♣ A Q
♠ A 7 6                             ♠ 8 4 3
♥ J 10 3                            ♥ A Q 9 8 7 5 4 2
♦ K J 7 5                           ♦ 8
♣ 8 6 3                             ♣ 5
                    ♠ Q
                    ♥ None
                    ♦ A Q 9 6 3
                    ♣ K J 10 9 7 4 2
```

North	East	South	West
1♠	4♥	5♣	All Pass

Opening lead: ♥J

75.

Instinctive Behavior

Animals survive on instinct, while man uses his powers of reasoning. That's why humans make better bridge players than, say, lions.

East took the ace of diamonds and saw that since two club tricks (at most) were available, the defense needed a heart trick. He thus shifted to hearts.

A lion would have led the jack, the top card of the doubleton, manely — I mean mainly — in deference to instinct. Actually, some defensive tendencies are so ingrained that even most humans follow them instinctively. This East, though, was on his toes; he led the seven of hearts!

Club Finesse

West covered South's eight with the nine. South won dummy's king, drew trumps and led a club to finesse with the nine. West took the queen and led another heart to the ace. When West got back in with the ace of clubs, he cashed the queen of hearts to defeat the contract.

South is safe if East succumbs to animal instinct and leads the jack of hearts. When West wins the queen of clubs, he can't continue hearts effectively, and South has time to set up the clubs and discard his losing hearts.

BIDDING QUIZ

You hold: ♠ 5 2 ♥ J 7 ♦ A Q J 4 2 ♣ 6 5 4 2. Your partner opens one club, you respond one diamond, and he next bids one spade. The opponents pass. What do you say?

ANSWER: To rebid the diamonds is risky; partner will be obliged to pass with a minimum hand and a singleton diamond. Return to two clubs. Partner has four or more clubs unless his distribution is precisely 4-3-3-3 (and then he may be able to continue by bidding two diamonds).

```
Dlr: North        ♠ A K 9 6
Vul: N-S          ♥ A K 3
                  ♦ 6 5
                  ♣ J 10 8 3
♠ 8 4                            ♠ 5 2
♥ Q 9 6 2                        ♥ J 7
♦ 9 8 7 3                        ♦ A Q J 4 2
♣ A Q 7                          ♣ 6 5 4 2
                  ♠ Q J 10 7 3
                  ♥ 10 8 5 4
                  ♦ K 10
                  ♣ K 9
```

North	East	South	West
1♣	1♦	1♠	2♦
2♠	Pass	3♠	Pass
4♠	All Pass		

Opening lead: ♦9

76.

The Difference

When I'm asked the difference between an expert and an average player, I reply that an expert often ignores "rules."

Since expert South has 10 points, he can redouble at his first turn. "But then," he thinks, "the opponents may compete vigorously in clubs or hearts, and I won't have room to bid my spades and also show my diamond support." South therefore begins to describe his hand immediately by responding one spade, and he lands in game after North raises.

East takes the A-Q of hearts and ace of clubs and leads a heart to dummy's king. South then leads the ace and a low spade.

Not Tempted

When East follows low, South isn't tempted to rely on "eight ever, nine never". He recalls that East doubled one diamond, promising length in the other suits, and finesses successfully with the jack of spades.

"Eight ever" is also a poor guide in diamonds. After the double, East is much more likely to have a singleton diamond than Q-x. South thus takes the king of diamonds and finesses with the jack. By thinking for himself, he makes game when an average player goes down two.

BIDDING QUIZ

You hold: ♠ K J 9 4 3 ♥ 10 5 ♦ K 10 5 3 ♣ K 4. Your partner opens 1NT, you respond three spades, and he next bids four clubs. The opponents pass. What do you say?

ANSWER: Your partner has spade support; without it, he would always return to 3NT. His unexpected rebid promises a fine spade fit, a maximum hand, the ace of clubs and slam interest. Since you have only 10 points, you aren't interested. Sign off at four spades.

Dlr: North	♠ A 7 5 2
Vul: None	♥ K J 4
	♦ A J 7 4 2
	♣ J

♠ 10	♠ Q 8 6
♥ 9 8 3 2	♥ A Q 7 6
♦ Q 8 6	♦ 9
♣ Q 10 8 6 3	♣ A 9 7 5 2

♠ K J 9 4 3
♥ 10 5
♦ K 10 5 3
♣ K 4

North	East	South	West
1♦	Dbl	1♠	Pass
3♠	Pass	4♠	All Pass

Opening lead: ♥9

77.

Dlr: West
Vul: None

♠ J 9 3
♥ J 7 5 2
♦ A Q 4
♣ K 9 4

♠ 8 6
♥ A K 10 9 6 3
♦ 5 2
♣ Q 10 3

West	North	East	South
1 NT	Pass	2♦	2♥
Pass	4♥	All Pass	

West leads the ♠K and continues with the ♠Q and ♠A. After ruffing, how should South continue? (West's 1 NT opening shows 16 to 18 points.)

78.

Dlr: South
Vul: N-S

♠ A J 5
♥ K 7
♦ 6 4 2
♣ K 10 7 5 2

♠ Q 4
♥ A Q 3 2
♦ Q J 8
♣ A J 9 3

South	West	North	East
1 NT	Pass	3 NT	All Pass

West leads the ♥J. Plan the play.

79.

Dlr: East
Vul: N-S

♠ K 10 7 5
♥ A J 6 5
♦ Q 10 6 5
♣ 9

```
      N
   W     E
      S
```

♠ 6 2
♥ K 10
♦ A K 9 8 4 2
♣ A 10 7

East	South	West	North
1♦	1♠	Pass	3♠
Pass	4♠	All Pass	

West leads the ♦3. Plan the defense.

80.

Dlr: West
Vul: N-S

♠ J 9 5 2
♥ Q 6 4
♦ A 8 2
♣ 10 7 2

♠ K Q 10 8 4 3
♥ A K J
♦ Q J
♣ J 8

West	North	East	South
Pass	Pass	Pass	1♠
2♣	2♠	Pass	4♠
All Pass			

West leads the ♣K and continues with the ♣Q and ♣A. East follows. After ruffing, how do you continue?

77.

Delay the Guess!

Procrastination (the word comes from the Latin *cras*, meaning *tomorrow*, for you etymologists) is a popular vice. At bridge, vice can easily become virtue.

South ruffed the third spade and hastily drew trumps. He then led a club ("Never put off until Trick Ten what you can do at Trick Six") and played dummy's king, expecting West to have the ace for his 1NT opening. East won, and though the diamond finesse worked for South later, West got the jack of clubs to defeat the contract.

Ruffs Diamond

It can be rewarding to procrastinate, and South should therefore put off the crucial guess in clubs. At the sixth trick, he must lead a diamond to finesse with dummy's queen. South next takes the ace of diamonds and ruffs a diamond.

South can then work out the club position. West has produced 15 high-card points (A-K-Q of spades, queen of hearts, K-J of diamonds). If West had the ace of clubs, his hand would be too strong to open 1NT; if he lacked the jack of clubs, his hand would be too weak.

South thus leads a club and finesses with dummy's nine, proving that vice is virtue, not vice-versa.

BIDDING QUIZ

You hold: ♠ 10 7 5 2 ♥ 8 ♦ 10 9 8 7 6 ♣ A 8 6. Your partner opens one spade, and the next player doubles. What do you say?

ANSWER: Bid three spades, a preemptive response that may stop the opponents from finding their fit in hearts. If they try four hearts anyway, your bid may encourage partner to take a good sacrifice. If you had a strong hand, you would redouble before supporting spades.

```
Dlr: West          ♠ J 9 3
Vul: None          ♥ J 7 5 2
                   ♦ A Q 4
                   ♣ K 9 4
♠ A K Q 4                          ♠ 10 7 5 2
♥ Q 4                              ♥ 8
♦ K J 3                            ♦ 10 9 8 7 6
♣ J 7 5 2                          ♣ A 8 6
                   ♠ 8 6
                   ♥ A K 10 9 6 3
                   ♦ 5 2
                   ♣ Q 10 3
```

West	North	East	South
1 NT	Pass	2♦	2♥
Pass	4♥	All Pass	

Opening lead: ♠K

78.

Louie's Lament

Unlucky Louie approached me with still another tale of woe. He wanted reassurance that he really is the world's unluckiest player.

In the deal below, Louie took the king of hearts at the first trick and led the ace and a low club. When West discarded, Louie put up dummy's king and gave up a club to East's queen.

Back came a diamond, and Louie's jack lost to the king. My ill-fated friend won the heart return and tried a spade finesse. East won and led another diamond, giving West three more tricks. Down two.

Good Defense

"My luck is really terrible," Louie moaned. "Clubs split three-one, and the king of spades and A-K of diamonds were all wrong. The opponents defended correctly too. Now what do you think of that?"

Well, I thought that if my luck were that bad, I'd try to play the dummy a little better. After winning the first trick, Louie should take the king of clubs and finesse with the jack.

This play produces an easy overtrick as the cards lie, but even if West had the queen of clubs, not even Louie could lose the contract. East could get in only once for a diamond lead before Louie set up his nine tricks.

BIDDING QUIZ

You hold: ♠ A J 5 ♥ K 7 ♦ 6 4 2 ♣ K 10 7 5 2. Your partner opens one heart, you respond two clubs, and he rebids two hearts. The opponents pass. What do you say?

ANSWER: Partner expects another bid from you, since your first response promised at least 10 points. A bid of 2NT is flawed, since you have no diamond strength. A raise to three hearts is best, though you would prefer to have three-card support. Maybe partner will hold a sixth heart.

```
Dlr: South          ♠ A J 5
Vul: N-S            ♥ K 7
                    ♦ 6 4 2
                    ♣ K 10 7 5 2

♠ 9 7 3 2                          ♠ K 10 8 6
♥ J 10 9 6                         ♥ 8 5 4
♦ A K 9 3                          ♦ 10 7 5
♣ 6                                ♣ Q 8 4

                    ♠ Q 4
                    ♥ A Q 3 2
                    ♦ Q J 8
                    ♣ A J 9 3
```

South	West	North	East
1 NT	Pass	3 NT	All Pass

Opening lead: ♥J

79.

Killing a Discard

Sometimes the defenders must deny declarer his tricks to make sure they get their own.

When the deal below appeared in a duplicate game, the contract at every table was four spades. Most of the East players won the first trick with the king of diamonds and continued with the ace and a low diamond. South ruffed with the ace of trumps, drew trumps, threw his low heart on the good queen of diamonds and led a club. East's ace of clubs won the last trick for the defense. Making four.

Returns Nine

A few Easts saw the need to set up a trick with the king of hearts before it was too late; they returned the nine of diamonds at the second trick. West ruffed and led a heart, obeying East's suit-preference signal.

South won the ace, however, accurately cashed only one high trump, and led the queen of diamonds to ruff out East's ace. South got back to dummy with a trump, took the ten of diamonds for a heart discard and led a club. Making four again.

The only East to beat the game led the deuce of diamonds at the second trick. West ruffed and returned a club to the ace, and East then led another low diamond. South had to ruff, and dummy's possible discard was eliminated. South lost a heart in the end.

BIDDING QUIZ

You hold: ♠ K 10 7 5 ♥ A J 6 5 ♦ Q 10 6 5 ♣ 9. Dealer, at your right, opens one club. You pass, and the next player bids one heart. Your partner doubles, and opener raises to two hearts. What do you say?

ANSWER: Cue-bid three hearts or jump to four spades. Partner asked you to bid diamonds or spades, and he has an opening bid or more to enter the auction between two bidding opponents. The hands fit well — partner is short in hearts, you are short in clubs — and game should make easily.

```
Dlr: East          ♠ K 10 7 5
Vul: N-S           ♥ A J 6 5
                   ♦ Q 10 6 5
                   ♣ 9
♠ 4 3                              ♠ 6 2
♥ 9 8 7 4 2                        ♥ K 10
♦ 3                                ♦ A K 9 8 4 2
♣ J 8 6 5 4                        ♣ A 10 7
                   ♠ A Q J 9 8
                   ♥ Q 3
                   ♦ J 7
                   ♣ K Q 3 2
```

East	South	West	North
1♦	1♠	Pass	3♠
Pass	4♠	All Pass	

Opening lead: ♦3

80.

When the Odds Change

Finesses start out as 50-50 possibilities, but circumstances can change the odds; a finesse may be a 1-99 proposition.

South in the deal below ruffed the third club and led a trump. East took the ace and got out with a heart. South won the ace, drew trumps, and led the queen of diamonds for a finesse that had no prayer of winning. East took the king to defeat the contract.

"My finesses never win," South groaned.

"Nor mine," said North, "especially when they have a zero percent chance. West passed as dealer and held A-K-Q-x-x of clubs. How could he have a side king?"

Ruff-sluff

"After you ruff the third club," North went on, "cash three heart tricks and lead dummy's jack of spades. Even if East has A-x, he may play low. Since he actually has the singleton ace, he must win and either lead a diamond from his king or give you a ruff-sluff."

"And what if the third heart gets ruffed?" South asked.

"Then you're always down," North replied. "An endplay is the only chance. The odds are poor, but the odds of winning a diamond finesse are nil."

BIDDING QUIZ

You hold: ♠ A ♥ 10 8 5 3 ♦ K 9 6 4 3 ♣ 6 4 3. Your partner opens one spade, you respond 1NT, and he next bids two clubs. The opponents pass. What do you say?

ANSWER: Pass. This has the makings of a trouble hand. Partner holds at most 18 points — with more he would have jumped to three clubs — and will often have 12 or 13. Since your side apparently lacks a good fit, get out while you have a chance to go plus.

```
Dlr: West              ♠ J 9 5 2
Vul: N-S               ♥ Q 6 4
                       ♦ A 8 2
                       ♣ 10 7 2

♠ 7 6                               ♠ A
♥ 9 7 2                             ♥ 10 8 5 3
♦ 10 7 5                            ♦ K 9 6 4 3
♣ A K Q 9 5                         ♣ 6 4 3

                       ♠ K Q 10 8 4 3
                       ♥ A K J
                       ♦ Q J
                       ♣ J 8
```

West	North	East	South
Pass	Pass	Pass	1♠
2♣	2♠	Pass	4♠
All Pass			

Opening lead: ♣K

81.

♠ J 8 6
♥ J 7 5 3
♦ 10 4
♣ K J 6 2

South	West	North	East
1♠	Pass	2♥	Pass
2♠	Pass	4♠	All Pass

What should West lead?

82.

Dlr: South   ♠ 8 4
Vul: N-S   ♥ K J 5
               ♦ 6 3 2
               ♣ A K 9 4 2

♠ Q 9 6 2
♥ A 7 3
♦ A K 5 4
♣ Q 8

South	West	North	East
1♦	Pass	2♣	Pass
2 NT	Pass	3 NT	All Pass

West leads the ♥2, and dummy's jack wins. How do you continue?

83.

Dlr: West
Vul: None

♠ 5 4
♥ A Q 7 4
♦ J 6 5 3
♣ 8 5 3

♠ K J 2
♥ J 10 8 5 3 2
♦ A K 10
♣ Q

West	North	East	South
Pass	Pass	Pass	1♥
Pass	2♥	Pass	3♥
All Pass			

West leads the ♣K and ♣A. After ruffing, how do you continue?

84.

Dlr: South
Vul: N-S

♠ A 10 8
♥ 7 5 2
♦ 6 4
♣ J 10 9 5 4

♠ Q J 3 2
♥ A Q 4
♦ A J 5 3
♣ A K

South	West	North	East
2 NT	Pass	3 NT	All Pass

West leads the ♠5, and East plays the six under dummy's eight. Plan the play.

81.

Go with Your Best

A fireballing young pitcher tried to fool the batter with a slow curveball and gave up a long home run. His manager proffered this bit of baseball wisdom: "If he beats you, make him beat your best stuff."

West in the deal below could expect a strong heart suit in dummy. It was clear that South would set up hearts to throw losers, and the defenders thus needed tricks in a hurry. Nevertheless, West led from his weakness; he started with the ten of diamonds.

South won the jack, drew trumps, discarded two clubs on the top hearts and ruffed a heart. He got to dummy with the ace of diamonds and threw his last club on a good heart. Making seven!

Four Tricks

It makes a difference of four tricks if West goes with his best stuff (his best hope for fast tricks) and leads a club. East wins the ace and returns a club for West to take the jack and king.

Since the defenders obviously have no tricks in hearts or diamonds, West can't lose by leading the 13th club next. East ruffs with the ten, forcing a trump honor from the South hand and promoting West's jack of trumps for the setting trick.

BIDDING QUIZ

You hold: ♠ A K 9 7 5 3 ♥ 2 ♦ K J 5 ♣ Q 10 8. Dealer, at your right, opens one heart. What do you say?

ANSWER: Bid one spade. At one time, you would have been obliged to double for takeout. In modern bridge, an overcall does not deny the strength of a double; it promises a long suit. If the next player raises to two hearts, and two passes follow, you can then double for takeout.

```
Dlr: South          ♠ Q 4 2
Vul: N-S            ♥ A K Q 10 4
                    ♦ A 8
                    ♣ 7 5 3
♠ J 8 6                             ♠ 10
♥ J 7 5 3                           ♥ 9 8 6
♦ 10 4                              ♦ Q 9 7 6 3 2
♣ K J 6 2                           ♣ A 9 4
                    ♠ A K 9 7 5 3
                    ♥ 2
                    ♦ K J 5
                    ♣ Q 10 8
```

South	West	North	East
1♠	Pass	2♥	Pass
2♠	Pass	4♠	All Pass

Opening lead: ??

82.

Bridge at Bat

Baseball pundits say that great pitching will always overcome great hitting. At bridge, good dummy play can foil fine defense.

The deal below was played four times in a team event, and dummy's jack of hearts always won the first trick. Three Souths then took the A-K-Q of clubs and lost a club to East's ten.

One East continued hearts (the equivalent of walking declarer on four pitches), and South had nine tricks. Another East led the five of spades, thus blocking the plate — I mean blocking the suit — and setting up South's nine. Again, South got home.

Correct Spade

The third East shifted to the correct spade: the jack. West took South's queen with the ace, led a spade to East's king, and waited with the 10-7 behind South's 9-6. Down one.

At Table Four, though, good dummy play prevailed. South crossed the plate by leading a club to his eight at the second trick. This play established four club tricks while keeping East out of the lead. Since East had only one chance to lead spades through South's Q-9-6-2, the defense could not take four spade tricks, and the game was safe.

BIDDING QUIZ

You hold: ♠ 8 4 ♥ K J 5 ♦ 6 3 2 ♣ A K 9 4 2. Your partner opens one heart, you respond two clubs, and he next bids two spades. The opponents pass. What do you say?

ANSWER: Partner's "reverse" promises extra strength. Game is sure, and slam is possible. You could set the trump suit with a minimum bid of three hearts, but then partner would wonder about the quality of your support. Jump to four hearts, promising strong support.

```
Dlr: South          ♠ 8 4
Vul: N-S            ♥ K J 5
                    ♦ 6 3 2
                    ♣ A K 9 4 2
    ♠ A 10 7 3                      ♠ K J 5
    ♥ Q 10 8 2                      ♥ 9 6 4
    ♦ 10 8 7                        ♦ Q J 9
    ♣ J 3                           ♣ 10 7 6 5
                    ♠ Q 9 6 2
                    ♥ A 7 3
                    ♦ A K 5 4
                    ♣ Q 8
```

South	West	North	East
1♦	Pass	2♣	Pass
2 NT	Pass	3 NT	All Pass

Opening lead: ♥2

83.

Declarer at the Bat

South stepped up to the plate full of confidence. He ruffed West's ace of clubs at the second trick and led a heart to finesse with dummy's queen, losing to the singleton king for strike one. When East led back a spade, South put in his jack. West's queen won, and the umpire said, "Strike two".

East won the spade return with the ace and got out with a club. After ruffing and drawing trumps, South swung once more, trying a diamond finesse with his ten. A moment later he was trudging back to the dugout, a strikeout victim.

Meet The Ball

South moaned over losing three finesses in a row, but North was unsympathetic. "You were aiming for the fences," he grumbled. "Just try to meet the ball."

South must remember that his goal is only nine tricks. He assures the contract by taking the ace of hearts at the third trick. If the king doesn't fall, and West wins the next heart, South can be sure that East has the ace of spades. If West had two aces and two kings, he would have opened the bidding.

If instead East takes the king of hearts and leads a spade, South plays the king. If West can win the ace, South knows that East must hold the queen of diamonds, and again the contract is safe.

BIDDING QUIZ

You hold: ♠ Q 9 6 3 ♥ 9 6 ♦ Q 9 4 ♣ A K 10 2. Your partner opens one spade, and the next player passes. What do you say?

ANSWER: Bid two clubs. Since you're too strong for a single raise and too weak for a double raise, bid a new suit at the two level, promising at least 10 points, and support spades next. Even if you play the popular limit raises, it's better to suggest the location of your side strength instead of raising directly.

```
Dlr: West              ♠ 5 4
Vul: None              ♥ A Q 7 4
                       ♦ J 6 5 3
                       ♣ 8 5 3
    ♠ Q 9 6 3                          ♠ A 10 8 7
    ♥ 9 6                              ♥ K
    ♦ Q 9 4                            ♦ 8 7 2
    ♣ A K 10 2                         ♣ J 9 7 6 4
                       ♠ K J 2
                       ♥ J 10 8 5 3 2
                       ♦ A K 10
                       ♣ Q
```

West	North	East	South
Pass	Pass	Pass	1♥
Pass	2♥	Pass	3♥
All Pass			

Opening lead: ♣K

FRANK STEWART

84.

Second Hand Sneeze

When Snow White arrived, the seven dwarfs were elated. At last, they had enough players for team-of-four matches! The dwarfs could not know that Snow White was an expert, having been schooled in the game by none other than the Magic Mirror.

In the deal below, Snow White landed at 3NT when Happy, North, happily raised her 2NT opening. Ms. White put on dummy's eight of spades at the first trick and was about to follow with her deuce when she saw the dreaded specter of a poisoned apple. Instead, she hastily unblocked the jack.

The fair princess next took the A-K of clubs, finessed with dummy's ten of spades, forced out the queen of clubs and still had the ace of spades as an entry to the good clubs. Making three. (Such careful play reflected well, so to speak, on her mentor, the Mirror.)

Sleepy Slips

At the other table, Sleepy was declarer. (Sleepy opened 3NT, since North was Bashful; he would never have raised 2NT with a mere five points.) But Sleepy slipped when he let dummy's eight win the first spade. He next took the A-K of clubs and led his remaining low spade.

At that point, Sneezy, sitting West, emitted a forceful AH-CHOO, and the king of spades fell out of his hand and floated to the table. After that play, not even the wicked queen's magic could have salvaged the contract. Declarer's second entry to dummy had vanished, and eight tricks were the limit.

BIDDING QUIZ

You hold: ♠ K 9 7 5 4 ♥ K 10 6 ♦ Q 9 2 ♣ 8 7. Your partner opens one heart, and the next player passes. What do you say?

ANSWER: Raise to two hearts. A bid of one spade might cause complications; if partner next bid two of a minor, and you returned to two hearts, he would be unsure of your heart support.

```
Dlr: South          ♠ A 10 8
Vul: N-S            ♥ 7 5 2
                    ♦ 6 4
                    ♣ J 10 9 5 4

♠ K 9 7 5 4                         ♠ 6
♥ K 10 6                            ♥ J 9 8 3
♦ Q 9 2                            ♦ K 10 8 7
♣ 8 7                              ♣ Q 6 3 2

                    ♠ Q J 3 2
                    ♥ A Q 4
                    ♦ A J 5 3
                    ♣ A K
```

South	West	North	East
2 NT	Pass	3 NT	All Pass

Opening lead: ♠5

85.

Dlr: South   ♠ 9 7 3
Vul: N-S   ♥ Q 10 6
              ♦ A K 6 2
              ♣ K 6 4

              ♠ K 6 4
              ♥ A K J 9 8
              ♦ 7 4 3
              ♣ A J

South	West	North	East
1♥	Pass	2♦	Pass
2 NT	Pass	3♥	Pass
4♥	All Pass		

West leads a trump. Plan the play.

86.

Dlr: South   ♠ 10 6 5
Vul: Both   ♥ J 8 5 3
              ♦ A 9 2
              ♣ K 7 4

♠ K J 9 7 4 3
♥ A
♦ Q 6 3
♣ J 9 3

```
      N
 W        E
      S
```

South	West	North	East
1♥	1♠	2♥	Pass
3♥	Pass	4♥	All Pass

You lead the ♠7. East produces the ace and returns the ♠2.
South follows with the eight and queen. How do you defend?

87.

Dlr: South   ♠ Q 9 6 4 3
Vul: N-S   ♥ A
             ♦ K J 5 2
             ♣ J 9 3

```
        N
      W   E      ♠ J
        S        ♥ K 9 6 3
                 ♦ Q 10 8 7 6
                 ♣ K 10 8
```

South	West	North	East
1♣	3♥	Pass	4♥
4♠	Pass	6♠	All Pass

West leads the ♥Q to dummy's ace. Declarer cashes the A-K of trumps, West following with the eight and ten. What should East discard?

88.

Dlr: North   ♠ K J 3
Vul: N-S   ♥ A K 7 6 2
             ♦ Q 3
             ♣ A J 6

             ♠ A 10 4
             ♥ 4 3
             ♦ K J 10 9 7 4
             ♣ 8 3

North	East	South	West
1♥	Pass	1 NT	Pass
2 NT	Pass	3 NT	All Pass

West leads the ♠5. Plan the play.

85.

Where Is Justice?

Bridge has no Justice Dept. to punish errors, or an august panel of justices to hear appeals. Bridge justice is blind.

South in the deal below drew trumps and, perhaps thinking that justice delayed is justice denied, immediately led a spade from dummy to finesse with his king. Justice was served when the defenders took three spade tricks, and East then led the jack of diamonds.

South won the ace and led a club to finesse with the jack, hoping to establish a discard for a low diamond. West took the queen and led another diamond, stranding declarer with a diamond loser. Down two.

Timing

"No justice," South groused. Actually, good timing will earn him a just reward.

South should win the first trick in dummy and finesse with the jack of clubs. West wins and leads a second trump. South takes the ace, cashes the ace of clubs and A-K of diamonds, throws his last diamond on the king of clubs and ruffs a diamond. When diamonds break 3-3, South can draw trumps and take dummy's last diamond for his tenth trick.

If diamonds break 4-2, South leads toward the king of spades as a last resort.

BIDDING QUIZ

You hold: ♠ Q J 10 5 ♥ 5 4 ♦ J 10 9 ♣ 10 7 5 2. Your partner opens 2NT, and the next player passes. What do you say?

ANSWER: Partner promises at least 21 points with balanced distribution, and you have three tens to go with your four points. Bid three clubs, Stayman. If partner obliges with a bid of three spades, raise to four spades; if he bids three diamonds (denying a four-card major) or three hearts, try 3NT.

```
Dlr: South        ♠ 9 7 3
Vul: N-S          ♥ Q 10 6
                  ♦ A K 6 2
                  ♣ K 6 4
♠ A 8 2                          ♠ Q J 10 5
♥ 7 3 2                          ♥ 5 4
♦ Q 8 5                          ♦ J 10 9
♣ Q 9 8 3                        ♣ 10 7 5 2
                  ♠ K 6 4
                  ♥ A K J 9 8
                  ♦ 7 4 3
                  ♣ A J
```

South	West	North	East
1♥	Pass	2♦	Pass
2 NT	Pass	3♥	Pass
4♥	All Pass		

Opening lead: ♥2

86.

Unwanted Gift

A certain Indian rajah would present an albino elephant to any courtier who annoyed him. The poor courtier was stuck with something that cost a fortune to maintain, but that he dared not get rid of. West in the deal below was luckier; he had a chance to unload his white elephant.

West did well to lead a spade against South's heart game. East won the ace and returned a spade to the queen and king. West then showed an odd affinity for his white elephant by leading the jack of spades.

Must Cash Ace

South ruffed, cashed the top clubs, ruffed a club and led the queen of hearts. This small deception wasn't needed; West had to win the singleton ace of hearts and was end-played. Another spade lead would concede a fatal ruff-sluff, and a diamond would let South pick up the diamonds without losing a trick.

West should see the impending danger. He must unload his white elephant by cashing the ace of hearts at the third trick, thus avoiding the chance of being thrown in.

Maybe West would have defended better — dare I say it? — if the contract had been three notrunk.

BIDDING QUIZ

You hold: ♠ A 2 ♥ 9 4 ♦ J 8 5 4 ♣ Q 10 8 6 2. Your partner opens one spade, you respond 1NT, and he next bids two hearts. The opponents pass. What do you say?

ANSWER: Bid two spades. Partner has five or more spades, but may have only four hearts. Take a preference, returning to the suit in which you have more trumps. Your hand is too weak to bid 2NT, which would promise a super-maximum 1NT response.

```
Dlr: South          ♠ 10 6 5
Vul: Both           ♥ J 8 5 3
                    ♦ A 9 2
                    ♣ K 7 4
♠ K J 9 7 4 3                        ♠ A 2
♥ A                                  ♥ 9 4
♦ Q 6 3                              ♦ J 8 5 4
♣ J 9 3                              ♣ Q 10 8 6 2
                    ♠ Q 8
                    ♥ K Q 10 7 6 2
                    ♦ K 10 7
                    ♣ A 5
```

South	West	North	East
1♥	1♠	2♥	Pass
3♥	Pass	4♥	All Pass

Opening lead: ♠7

87.

Weighty Matters

South took dummy's ace of hearts at the first trick and drew trumps. East discarded a heart. Declarer then led a diamond toward dummy and put up the king when West impassively followed low. Although South eventually lost a club trick to East, the slam was safe.

East landed on his partner like a ton of bricks. "If you had a grain of sense," he pounded away at West, "you'd have taken your ace. Why play low when you know declarer has a black two-suiter?"

Only Chance

"What a twenty-four-carat misanalysis!" West retorted. "What if declarer had only five clubs to the A-Q-10 and two diamonds? Then our only chance is for me to play low on the diamond lead to make him guess."

I can sympathize with West. Only East knew that the defenders had a surprise club trick coming. Since the setting trick could only be the ace of diamonds, East should discard the queen of diamonds at the third trick, compelling his partner to take the ace.

Which goes to show that an ounce of prevention has lost none of its value.

BIDDING QUIZ

You hold: ♠ A K 7 5 2 ♥ 5 ♦ 4 ♣ A Q 7 6 4 2. Dealer, at your right, opens one heart. What do you say?

ANSWER: Avoid a takeout double with such wild distribution. Since the opponents may compete vigorously in hearts or diamonds, you must start to bid your suits. Bid two clubs first. If the next player jumps to four hearts, for instance, you can bid four spades at your next turn and play game at spades or clubs.

Dlr: South	♠ Q 9 6 4 3	
Vul: N-S	♥ A	
	♦ K J 5 2	
	♣ J 9 3	

♠ 10 8		♠ J
♥ Q J 10 8 7 4 2		♥ K 9 6 3
♦ A 9 3		♦ Q 10 8 7 6
♣ 5		♣ K 10 8

	♠ A K 7 5 2	
	♥ 5	
	♦ 4	
	♣ A Q 7 6 4 2	

South	West	North	East
1♣	3♥	Pass	4♥
4♠	Pass	6♠	All Pass

Opening lead: ♥Q

88.

Bridge Skies Crowded

The great Scottish bridge writer Hugh Kelsey uses a picturesque phrase to account for inexplicable lapses in concentration. Kelsey says, "A cow flew by." South in the deal below obviously had cow trouble.

South's prospects in 3NT looked good when East led a spade, but then the flying cow put in an appearance. Distracted by the airborne bovine, South played a low spade from dummy, and the contract sailed out the window along with the cow.

Plays Low

East put up the queen of spades, and declarer suddenly realized that if he won the ace, he would have no entry to the critical diamond suit. Cowed by this unforeseen development, South ducked the first trick(!), hoping for a spade continuation. East found the good shift to a low club, however. South then had to go down and he lapsed into a bad "moooood" for the rest of the evening.

If South ignores the flying cow, he will play dummy's jack (or king) of spades at the first trick. Whatever East does, South retains a spade entry to his hand. South can set up and cash his diamonds and take no fewer than 11 tricks.

BIDDING QUIZ

You hold: ♠ K J 3 ♥ A K 7 6 2 ♦ Q 3 ♣ A J 6. Your partner opens one diamond, you respond one heart, and he next bids 1NT. The opponents pass. What do you say?

ANSWER: Bid 4NT to invite slam (not to ask for aces). Partner has 13 to 15 points, and your hand is worth 19. He will go to 6NT with 15 points, pass with 13 and use his judgment with 14. To bid 6NT yourself is aggressive; partner may have A-Q-x of spades, wasting one of your points.

```
Dlr: North          ♠ K J 3
Vul: N-S            ♥ A K 7 6 2
                    ♦ Q 3
                    ♣ A J 6
  ♠ 9 7 6 5 2                        ♠ Q 8
  ♥ 8 5                              ♥ Q J 10 9
  ♦ A 2                              ♦ 8 6 5
  ♣ K 9 5 2                          ♣ Q 10 7 4
                    ♠ A 10 4
                    ♥ 4 3
                    ♦ K J 10 9 7 4
                    ♣ 8 3
```

North	East	South	West
1♥	Pass	1 NT	Pass
2 NT	Pass	3 NT	All Pass

Opening lead: ♠5

89.

Dlr: South   ♠ Q 5 4
Vul: N-S   ♥ 9 3 2
               ♦ A J 10
               ♣ 8 5 4 2

               ♠ A J
               ♥ A K Q 8 5 4
               ♦ K
               ♣ A K Q J

South	West	North	East
2♥	Pass	3♥	Pass
4 NT	Pass	5♦	Pass
7♥	All Pass		

West leads the ♦9. Plan the play.

90.

Dlr: South   ♠ Q J 9 4 2
Vul: N-S   ♥ A 10 4
               ♦ Q 7
               ♣ 6 4 2

               ♠ K
               ♥ K J 2
               ♦ A 6 5 4 2
               ♣ A K Q J

South	West	North	East
1♦	Pass	1♠	Pass
3♣	Pass	3♠	Pass
3 NT	All Pass		

West leads the ♣10. Plan the play.

91.

Dlr: South   ♠ K Q 7
Vul: N-S   ♥ K 6 4
            ♦ 8 5 2
            ♣ A 10 7 3

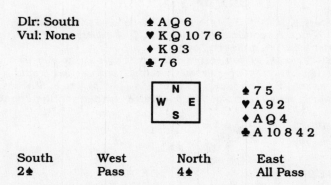

                    ♠ A 10 6 2
                    ♥ 9 8 3
                    ♦ 10 7 6
                    ♣ K 9 2

South	West	North	East
1 NT	Pass	3 NT	All Pass

West leads the ♥2. Declarer wins in his hand with the queen and leads the ♣J, losing to your king. How do you defend?

92.

Dlr: South   ♠ A Q 6
Vul: None   ♥ K Q 10 7 6
            ♦ K 9 3
            ♣ 7 6

                    ♠ 7 5
                    ♥ A 9 2
                    ♦ A Q 4
                    ♣ A 10 8 4 2

South	West	North	East
2♠	Pass	4♠	All Pass

South's 2♠ opening is a weak two-bid, promising about 10 high-card points and a six-card suit. West leads the ♣Q, and South drops the king under your ace. How do you continue?

89.

Don't Blow Big Chance

The *Official Encyclopedia of Bridge* says that you'll hold 27 high-card points once in every 20,000 deals. Nothing could be sadder than going down when you finally pick up such a monster.

South won the first trick with the king of diamonds and took two high hearts, hoping for a 2-2 split and an entry to dummy with the third trump. When West discarded, South ran his winners, hoping the defenders would take a siesta. Of course, East's king of spades won the last trick.

"I had twenty-seven points," moaned the shattered declarer.

"You'd have been better off with twenty-four," North remarked.

Wins In Dummy

South would surely succeed if his king of diamonds were a low diamond. He should win the opening lead with dummy's ace, crashing his king, and finesse with the jack of spades. This play gives him a 45% chance for the contract (the finesse is a 50-50 proposition, but trumps may split 4-0). The actual play offered only about a 36% chance.

"Cheer up," North ungenerously turned the knife. "It'll be only twenty thousand more deals before you hold a hand that good again."

BIDDING QUIZ

You hold: ♠ K 10 8 ♥ J 7 6 ♦ Q 6 5 3 2 ♣ 10 3. Your partner opens one club, you respond one diamond, and he rebids one spade. The opponents pass. What do you say?

ANSWER: Pass. After you respond in a new suit at the one level, a non-jump change of suit by opener isn't forcing. Your partner would have bid two spades if he had enough to offer a play for game. Since you were barely worth your first response, don't give partner another chance.

```
Dlr: South          ♠ Q 5 4
Vul: N-S            ♥ 9 3 2
                    ♦ A J 10
                    ♣ 8 5 4 2
♠ 9 7 6 3 2                         ♠ K 10 8
♥ 10                                ♥ J 7 6
♦ 9 8 7 4                           ♦ Q 6 5 3 2
♣ 9 7 6                             ♣ 10 3
                    ♠ A J
                    ♥ A K Q 8 5 4
                    ♦ K
                    ♣ A K Q J
```

South	West	North	East
2♥	Pass	3♥	Pass
4 NT	Pass	5♦	Pass
7♥	All Pass		

Opening lead: ♦9

90.

Not Enough Points

Long ago, theorists found that 26 points often produce exactly nine tricks at notrump. In the deal below, South had points to spare, but still lost his game.

After winning the first club, South led the king of spades. West played low. South then took his remaining clubs and tried to find the queen of hearts for a ninth trick. When he led a heart to finesse with dummy's ten, though, East won the queen.

South took the heart return in his hand and tried leading a diamond to dummy's queen. East won the king and led a third heart to dummy's ace. When South continued with the queen of spades, West took the ace, cashed a heart and led a diamond. South then lost a diamond to East in the end and went down one.

Creates Entry

"Sorry, partner," North deadpanned. "Maybe I should have had more points for you."

You'd think South could generate nine tricks with 30 points. He actually has several ways to succeed. The simplest is to lead the jack of hearts for a finesse at the third trick.

If the jack wins, South has at least nine tricks. If the jack loses to East, the ace and ten of hearts both become entries to dummy, letting South establish and cash a second spade trick.

BIDDING QUIZ

You hold: ♠ 10 8 7 6 ♥ Q 8 5 ♦ K J 9 8 ♣ 5 3. Your partner opens one heart, and the next player passes. What do you say?

ANSWER: Bid two hearts. On a few six-point hands, you might discourage partner by responding 1NT even with three-card heart support. Here you have fair hearts, a possible ruffing value and concentrated side values. Avoid a one-spade response; you need not suggest another trump suit when a heart fit exists.

```
Dlr: South            ♠ Q J 9 4 2
Vul: N-S              ♥ A 10 4
                      ♦ Q 7
                      ♣ 6 4 2
  ♠ A 5 3                              ♠ 10 8 7 6
  ♥ 9 7 6 3                            ♥ Q 8 5
  ♦ 10 3                               ♦ K J 9 8
  ♣ 10 9 8 7                           ♣ 5 3
                      ♠ K
                      ♥ K J 2
                      ♦ A 6 5 4 2
                      ♣ A K Q J
```

South	West	North	East
1♦	Pass	1♠	Pass
3♣	Pass	3♠	Pass
3 NT	All Pass		

Opening lead: ♣10

91.

Listen to Reason

Bridge "rules" are like seductive voices whispering in your ear. Good players listen only to the sweet voice of reason.

South took the first heart in his hand with the queen and led the jack of clubs for a finesse. East won the king and heard a voice in each ear. "Return partner's heart lead," urged one. "Lead a diamond up to dummy's weakness," coaxed the other.

East finally led a heart. South took dummy's king, lost a diamond finesse, won the next heart, lost to the ace of spades and had ten tricks.

No Side Trick

East defeats 3NT if he ignores *both* voices. On the bidding, West can hold at most five high-card points. If West has strong hearts, he can't have a side trick; thus, a heart return won't defeat the contract.

West's lead of the deuce of hearts suggests four cards in hearts. Since West would instead lead a diamond with four good diamonds, a diamond return won't help the defense.

East must lead a spade, hoping West has the jack of spades plus an entry. South wins with dummy's queen and tries a diamond finesse. When West takes the king, a spade return gives the defense five tricks.

BIDDING QUIZ

You hold: ♠ A 10 6 2 ♥ 9 8 3 ♦ 10 7 6 ♣ K 9 2. Dealer, at your left, opens one heart. Your partner doubles, and the next player raises to two hearts. What do you say?

ANSWER: Bid two spades. Partner promises at least an opening bid and is almost sure to hold four cards in spades. If you don't compete, the opponents will be stealing you blind. Think of it this way: your partner "bid" spades when he doubled; you are merely raising him.

Dlr: South	♠ K Q 7	
Vul: N-S	♥ K 6 4	
	♦ 8 5 2	
	♣ A 10 7 3	

♠ J 8 4		♠ A 10 6 2
♥ J 10 5 2		♥ 9 8 3
♦ K 9 3		♦ 10 7 6
♣ 8 6 5		♣ K 9 2

	♠ 9 5 3	
	♥ A Q 7	
	♦ A Q J 4	
	♣ Q J 4	

South	West	North	East
1 NT	Pass	3 NT	All Pass

Opening lead: ♥2

92.

Don't Trust Bromides

Among the first rules of defensive play beginners learn is, "Lead through strength and up to weakness." In the deal below, East staked the defense on that bromide and found himself betrayed.

East's ace of clubs dropped South's king at the first trick. Observing the king of diamonds in dummy, East exited with a club. South ruffed, drew trumps and led the jack of hearts. East took the ace and wondered what to do next. Actually, he needed to cash the ace of diamonds just to hold South to no overtricks.

Must Attack

The defense obviously needs two diamond tricks to beat the game, and it is vital to establish them before South draws trumps and sets up the hearts. Since it is equally clear that West will never win a trick to lead a diamond through dummy, East must attack diamonds himself.

East's best lead at the second trick is the four of diamonds; this lead is sure to gain if West has the jack of diamonds and puts South to a tough guess if West has the ten.

On the actual deal, if South misguesses by playing a low diamond from his hand, West's ten forces dummy's king. When East takes the ace of hearts, he cashes the A-Q of diamonds to beat the contract.

BIDDING QUIZ

You hold: ♠ A Q 6 ♥ K Q 10 7 6 ♦ K 9 3 ♣ 7 6. You open one heart, and your partner responds one spade. The opponents pass. What do you say?

ANSWER: Bid two spades. It's not pleasant to raise with three trumps, but the alternatives are worse. A 1NT rebid with two low clubs is unattractive, and a rebid of two hearts would suggest a six-card suit. If partner passes your raise with four mediocre spades, you may survive; the contract will be only two.

```
Dlr: South          ♠ A Q 6
Vul: None           ♥ K Q 10 7 6
                    ♦ K 9 3
                    ♣ 7 6
♠ 8 3                               ♠ 7 5
♥ 5 4 3                             ♥ A 9 2
♦ 10 8 6                            ♦ A Q 4
♣ Q J 9 5 3                         ♣ A 10 8 4 2
                    ♠ K J 10 9 4 2
                    ♥ J 8
                    ♦ J 7 5 2
                    ♣ K
```

South	West	North	East
2♠	Pass	4♠	All Pass

Opening lead: ♣Q

93.

Dlr: South
Vul: N-S

```
              ♠ A 6 4
              ♥ 7 5 2
              ♦ K Q 10 9 4
              ♣ 8 2
                              ♠ 9 8
         ┌─────────┐         ♥ J 10 6 4
         │    N    │         ♦ A J 5
         │  W   E  │         ♣ 9 7 6 5
         │    S    │
         └─────────┘
```

South	West	North	East
1 NT	Pass	3 NT	All Pass

West leads the ♥3, and your ten loses to South's queen. South then leads the ♦2: six, king. Plan your defense.

94.

Dlr: East
Vul: N-S

```
              ♠ Q 5 2
              ♥ K 9
              ♦ 9 6 4 2
              ♣ K Q 5 4


              ♠ A 7 4
              ♥ Q J 10 7 5 4 2
              ♦ J
              ♣ 10 3
```

East	South	West	North
1 NT	2♥	2♠	3♥
All Pass			

West leads the ♣J. Plan the play.

95.

Dlr: North
Vul: N-S

♠ A
♥ K 10 5 2
♦ 7 6 4 3 2
♣ A Q 3

♠ K 5 2
♥ A Q 8 4 3
♦ K 10 9
♣ 4 2

North	East	South	West
1♦	Pass	1♥	Pass
2♥	Pass	4♥	All Pass

West leads the ♠Q. Plan the play.

96.

Dlr: South
Vul: N-S

♠ 5
♥ A K 4 2
♦ 7 5 2
♣ 7 6 4 3 2

♠ K Q J 10 9 6
♥ 3
♦ A Q 3
♣ A Q 5

South	West	North	East
1♠	Pass	1 NT	Pass
4♠	All Pass		

West leads the ♥Q. You take dummy's A-K to throw a club (not best, actually) and finesse with the ♣Q. West wins the king and forces you to ruff a heart. The ♠K goes to East's ace, and back comes the ♦6. How do you play?

93.

Declarer Beware!

South took the queen of hearts at the first trick and sat there in his chair, prepared to declare. With a confident air, he led a diamond and played dummy's king.

If East had taken the ace, South could have gotten home by finessing with the ten of diamonds next. But did East win the first diamond? Au contraire! And South's communications were thereby impaired.

Despite this scare, declarer was aware that his prospects were still fair. Playing with care, he got back to his hand with the ace of clubs and led another diamond to the queen and East's ace.

Spade Shift

South was still safe if East returned a heart, but East showed flair beyond compare; he switched to the nine of spades, and South's savoir-faire turned to despair.

South covered with the ten, and West's king forced the ace, leaving dummy without an entry. South then spared East a glare, gave the ceiling a stare, muttered a prayer and led a club to finesse with the jack. West won the queen (he did his share), and 3NT was beyond repair.

After this rare fare by the East-West pair, South was tearing his hair. Dare I say 'twas a defense extraordinaire'?

BIDDING QUIZ

You hold: ♠ K 7 5 2 ♥ K 9 8 3 ♦ 6 3 ♣ Q 10 3. Dealer, at your left, opens one club. Your partner doubles, and the next player passes. What do you say?

ANSWER: Plan ahead and bid one spade. The opponents are likely to compete in a minor suit. You can then bid hearts and play in the major suit your partner likes best. If you respond one heart and bid spades next, a contract of two hearts will be out of reach.

Dlr: South	♠ A 6 4	
Vul: N-S	♥ 7 5 2	
	♦ K Q 10 9 4	
	♣ 8 2	

♠ K 7 5 2		♠ 9 8
♥ K 9 8 3		♥ J 10 6 4
♦ 6 3		♦ A J 5
♣ Q 10 3		♣ 9 7 6 5

	♠ Q J 10 3	
	♥ A Q	
	♦ 8 7 2	
	♣ A K J 4	

South	West	North	East
1 NT	Pass	3 NT	All Pass

Opening lead: ♥3

94.

Conflicting Advice

"Draw trumps quickly so the defenders can't ruff your winners," the bridge teacher instructed. His pupil yawned.

"Delay drawing trumps," the sage continued, "to achieve the same goal." The pupil thought his master was a candidate for the men in the white coats until the deal below came along.

The pupil, South, played a low spade from dummy at the first trick and won the ace. The teacher nodded approval. Next, though, South led a trump. East took the ace, cashed the king of spades and led a diamond. West won and led a spade for East to ruff, and the ace of clubs provided the setting trick.

Has Entry

"This time you can't avoid a ruff by leading trumps," scolded the teacher. "West surely has an entry in diamonds. In that case, your only chance is to break the defenders' communication."

From that day on, the pupil paid closer attention when his mentor offered seemingly conflicting advice. If South leads a diamond at the second trick — killing West's entry before East can unblock the king of spades — the contract is safe.

BIDDING QUIZ

You hold: ♠ J 10 9 6 3 ♥ 6 ♦ A 8 7 5 ♣ J 9 2. Your partner opens one heart, you respond one spade, and he jumps to three hearts. The opponents pass. What do you say?

ANSWER: Partner promises about 17 high-card points with a good six- or seven-card suit. Although partner's bid is a strong game invitation, you couldn't have less for your first response, and your heart support is nil. Pass.

Dlr: East	♠ Q 5 2		
Vul: N-S	♥ K 9		
	♦ 9 6 4 2		
	♣ K Q 5 4		
♠ J 10 9 6 3		♠ K 8	
♥ 6		♥ A 8 3	
♦ A 8 7 5		♦ K Q 10 3	
♣ J 9 2		♣ A 8 7 6	
	♠ A 7 4		
	♥ Q J 10 7 5 4 2		
	♦ J		
	♣ 10 3		

East	South	West	North
1 NT	2♥	2♠	3♥
All Pass			

Opening lead: ♠J

95.

Play It as It Lies

In golf, a well-struck shot doesn't always find the green. At bridge, the dummy may not have perfect cards. Still, you must play the ball — or the dummy — as it lies.

Since South had help for the suit North bid, he expected to make game easily. The sight of North's scratchy diamonds was disconcerting, and South proceeded to misplay the hand.

He took the ace of spades, drew trumps and led a diamond to finesse with the nine. West won the jack and led a club. Dummy's queen lost to the king, and East's diamond return gave West two more tricks with the queen and ace. Down one.

Can Make Five

"I make five easily if your A-Q are in the suit you bid," South remarked.

"Play it as it lies," North replied. "You can make four anyway."

After South draws trumps, he takes the king of spades to pitch a club from dummy, ruffs a spade, cashes the ace of clubs and exits with queen of clubs for an endplay. East wins and must return a diamond to avoid giving South a ruff-sluff.

South plays the nine. West wins, but he must either take the ace of diamonds or concede a ruff-sluff. Either way, South gets his tenth trick.

BIDDING QUIZ

You hold: ♠ Q J 10 6 ♥ 9 6 ♦ A Q J ♣ 10 8 6 5. Dealer, at your left, opens one club. Your partner doubles, and the next player raises to two clubs. What do you say?

ANSWER: Bid three spades. You would compete with a bid of two spades ("raising" partner, in effect, since he "bid" spades when he doubled) if your Q-J of diamonds were low diamonds. Since partner has an opening bid or better with club shortness, game is possible.

```
Dlr: North          ♠ A
Vul: N-S            ♥ K 10 5 2
                    ♦ 7 6 4 3 2
                    ♣ A Q 3
♠ Q J 10 6                          ♠ 9 8 7 4 3
♥ 9 6                               ♥ J 7
♦ A Q J                             ♦ 8 5
♣ 10 8 6 5                          ♣ K J 9 7
                    ♠ K 5 2
                    ♥ A Q 8 4 3
                    ♦ K 10 9
                    ♣ 4 2
```

North	East	South	West
1♦	Pass	1♥	Pass
2♥	Pass	4♥	All Pass

Opening lead: ♠Q

96.

Murder, He Wrote

Someone was hauled away on a murder charge after the play of the deal below. Can you guess who the foul felon was?

South took dummy's top hearts to throw a club (a diamond discard would be slightly better play) and next tried a club finesse with the queen. West won the king and got out with a heart, forcing South to ruff.

South next led the king of spades to East's ace. When a low diamond came back, declarer tried another finesse with a queen. West won the king, and South lost a second diamond later to go down one.

Diamond Losers

Any jury would convict South of murdering the play. At the point when East led a diamond, the dummy was barren; if South had diamond losers, he had no way to avoid them. East surely had a safe exit available in hearts or trumps. Thus, the only reason East could have for leading a diamond was to let South take a finesse East knew would lose.

South should therefore rise with the ace of diamonds, draw trumps, and lead a low diamond as his best chance, hoping West started with K-x.

Who was the murderer? East was so insulted that South had played him for a horrible defensive error that he produced a blunt instrument from his coat and fatally bonked South on the noggin.

BIDDING QUIZ

You hold: ♠ 7 4 2 ♥ Q J 10 6 5 ♦ K 10 ♣ K 9 8. Your partner opens 2NT, and the next player passes. What do you say?

ANSWER: Bid three hearts. Since partner has promised great strength, any response is forcing to game. If partner raises to four hearts, bid five hearts, inviting slam. If he rebids 3NT, raise to 4NT as a quantitative slam try. (This 4NT bid, when your side hasn't found a trump suit, is not ace-asking.)

```
Dlr: South          ♠ 5
Vul: N-S            ♥ A K 4 2
                    ♦ 7 5 2
                    ♣ 7 6 4 3 2
  ♠ 7 4 2                           ♠ A 8 3
  ♥ Q J 10 6 5                      ♥ 9 8 7
  ♦ K 10                            ♦ J 9 8 6 4
  ♣ K 9 8                           ♣ J 10
                    ♠ K Q J 10 9 6
                    ♥ 3
                    ♦ A Q 3
                    ♣ A Q 5
```

South	West	North	East
1♠	Pass	1 NT	Pass
4♠	All Pass		

Opening lead: ♥Q

97.

Dlr: North   ♠ Q 5 4
Vul: N-S   ♥ K 7
               ♦ A 6 4 2
               ♣ A K 6 4

               ♠ A K 7 2
               ♥ A Q J 6 4 2
               ♦ None
               ♣ J 7 3

North	East	South	West
1 NT	Pass	3♥	Pass
3 NT	Pass	4♠	Pass
5♣	Pass	6♥	Pass
7♥	All Pass		

West leads the ♦K. Plan the play.

98.

Dlr: South   ♠ A K 6 4
Vul: N-S   ♥ 6 5
               ♦ A J 4 3 2
               ♣ J 8

♠ J 7 2
♥ K Q 10 9 3   N
♦ K 9 8   W   E
♣ A 4   S

South	West	North	East
1♣	1♥	2♦	Pass
3♣	Pass	3♠	Pass
3 NT	All Pass		

You lead the ♥Q, which conventionally asks East to drop the
♥J if he has it. But the play to the first trick is: ♥Q, five,
deuce, seven. How do you continue?

99.

Dlr: South		♠ J 9 7 5 2	
Vul: N-S		♥ J 8	
		♦ K Q J 10	
		♣ K Q	

		♠ A Q	
		♥ A Q 10 9 6 2	
		♦ 7 5 2	
		♣ A 5	

South	West	North	East
1♥	Pass	1♠	Pass
4♥(!)	Pass	4 NT	Pass
5♠	Pass	6♥	All Pass

West leads the ♣J. Plan the play.

100.

Dlr: South		♠ A K 4 2	
Vul: N-S		♥ 7 5 2	
		♦ 8 6 3	
		♣ 8 6 3	

		♠ 6	
		♥ A K 9 6 4	
		♦ A 7 2	
		♣ A K 4 2	

South	West	North	East
1♥	Pass	2♥	Pass
4♥	All Pass		

West leads the ♠J. Plan the play.

97.

Timing Is the Essence

Declarers often play too fast to the first trick, but at a grand slam you'd think South would have known better.

North's bid of seven hearts was risky; North certainly could not count 13 tricks, and for all he knew, South's bid of six hearts might itself have been a bit of a gamble.

South took only a few seconds to assure defeat. Spotting the ace of diamonds in dummy, he impulsively used it to win the first trick. He then thought long and hard about what to discard from his hand and finally threw his club "loser". The slam could no longer be made.

Delays Discard

Since South cannot be sure what he should discard on the ace of diamonds, he should ruff the first trick. South then draws trumps and cashes the A-K of clubs.

When West queen falls, South wins the 13th trick with the jack of clubs. If the queen did not fall, South would discard the jack of clubs on the ace of diamonds and ruff a club. If clubs broke 3-3, dummy's fourth club would fulfill the contract. If not, South would still have the chance of a 3-3 break in spades or a spade-club squeeze.

Just a moment's reflection at the first trick: that was all South needed to bring home the slam.

BIDDING QUIZ

You hold: ♠ J 9 8 3 ♥ 9 5 3 ♦ K Q J 9 ♣ Q 2. Your partner opens one diamond. The next player passes. What do you say?

ANSWER: Bid one spade. You must suppress your diamond help temporarily to search for a major-suit fit. Partner will allow for a poor four-card spade suit and will seldom raise without four-card support. If he next bids, say, two clubs, you'll unveil your diamond support.

```
Dlr: North          ♠ Q 5 4
Vul: N-S            ♥ K 7
                    ♦ A 6 4 2
                    ♣ A K 6 4
♠ J 9 8 3                        ♠ 10 6
♥ 9 5 3                          ♥ 10 8
♦ K Q J 9                        ♦ 10 8 7 5 3
♣ Q 2                            ♣ 10 9 8 5
                    ♠ A K 7 2
                    ♥ A Q J 6 4 2
                    ♦ None
                    ♣ J 7 3
```

North	East	South	West
1 NT	Pass	3♥	Pass
3 NT	Pass	4♣	Pass
5♣	Pass	6♥	Pass
7♥	All Pass		

Opening lead: ♦K

98.

South Takes a Bath

In the deal below, West started with the queen of hearts against 3NT. This was a conventional lead, much favored by experts, that asked East to play the jack of hearts if he held it. East instead followed with the deuce, and South offered his seven, executing an ancient maneuver known as the "Bath Coup."

West knew that South surely had the A-J of hearts left, and another heart lead would give away a trick. Nevertheless, West continued with a suicidal-looking ten of hearts. Declarer eyed this card with distaste; communication with his hand had been dealt a blow.

Spade Shift

South took the jack of hearts and attacked clubs. West refused the first club, won the second with his ace and shifted to a spade. South won dummy's king and tried to reach his hand with the queen of diamonds. West took the king and led another spade to the ace.

South then cashed four diamond tricks, but that was the end for him; East won the last two tricks with high spades.

No other play would work for poor South. If he concedes a diamond early, the defense can afford to clear the hearts. Nor would it help South to win the first trick. He just has to take a bath, compliments of West's "anti-Bath Coup."

BIDDING QUIZ

You hold: ♠ J 7 2 ♥ K Q 10 9 3 ♦ K 9 8 ♣ A 4. You open one heart, and your partner bids one spade. The opponents pass. What do you say?

ANSWER: Bid 1NT, promising balanced distribution with 13 to 15 points. Avoid a rebid of two hearts, which would suggest a six-card heart suit. When you open one heart, partner will expect a five-card suit no matter what you rebid.

```
Dlr: South          ♠ A K 6 4
Vul: N-S            ♥ 6 5
                    ♦ A J 4 3 2
                    ♣ J 8
♠ J 7 2                             ♠ Q 10 9 8
♥ K Q 10 9 3                        ♥ 8 4 2
♦ K 9 8                             ♦ 10 7 6
♣ A 4                              ♣ 7 5 3
                    ♠ 5 3
                    ♥ A J 7
                    ♦ Q 5
                    ♣ K Q 10 9 6 2
```

South	West	North	East
1♣	1♥	2♦	Pass
3♣	Pass	3♣	Pass
3 NT	All Pass		

Opening lead: ♥Q

99.

Feline Fine

South found himself catapulted into slam by North, although his own overbid of four hearts was the catalyst.

South, no caterpillar, played the slam quickly; he won dummy's queen of clubs at the first trick, drew trumps with two finesses and led a diamond. Catastrophe came when East won the third diamond and led a spade. Since South couldn't get to dummy's good diamond, he finessed with the queen, and West sat in the catbird seat with the king. Down one.

The play brought a cataclysm of catcalls from the kibitzers, plus a cataract of carping by North. "Not to be catty," North said, "but you were either catnapping or cataleptic. The catchword is timing. Win the first club in your hand with the ace and lead a diamond."

Correct

North's catechism was correct. If East takes the first diamond and leads a spade, South wins the ace, gets to dummy with the king of clubs, draws trumps and runs the diamonds to throw the queen of spades. If East refuses the first diamond, South draws trumps and sets up the diamonds while the king of clubs remains as an entry to dummy.

I can't sentence South to a taste of a cat-o'-nine-tails just because he botched a bridge hand, but I can suggest a catalog of books in the category of dummy play.

I chose a catchy title for this write-up, don't you think?

BIDDING QUIZ

You hold: ♠ J 9 7 5 2 ♥ J 8 ♦ K Q J 10 ♣ K Q. Your partner opens one diamond, you respond one spade, and he next bids two clubs. The opponents pass. What do you say?

ANSWER: Unless you play a jump preference in opener's minor as invitational, bid three diamonds. Otherwise, jump to four or five diamonds or force with a devious fourth-suit bid of two hearts.

```
Dlr: South          ♠ J 9 7 5 2
Vul: N-S            ♥ J 8
                    ♦ K Q J 10
                    ♣ K Q
  ♠ K 10 6 3                      ♠ 8 4
  ♥ 5 3                           ♥ K 7 4
  ♦ 9 3                           ♦ A 8 6 4
  ♣ J 10 9 6 2                    ♣ 8 7 4 3
                    ♠ A Q
                    ♥ A Q 10 9 6 2
                    ♦ 7 5 2
                    ♣ A 5
```

South	West	North	East
1♥	Pass	1♠	Pass
4♥(!)	Pass	4 NT	Pass
5♠	Pass	6♥	All Pass

Opening lead: ♣J

100.

Universal Truths

The Universe operates according to certain laws. (Some sages have surmised that the cosmos behaves as it does merely because otherwise we wouldn't be here to observe it!) Yet how dull life would be if suits always split as they're supposed to.

South took the A-K of spades to throw a diamond and next led the A-K and a low club. West won the ten, continued with the queen of clubs to let East overruff dummy, and later got a diamond trick and a trump. Down one.

"So much for odds," South sighed. "If clubs split four-two, the defender with two clubs will usually have three trumps. And it doesn't help me to take the A-K of hearts and then lead three rounds of clubs; West will wins and cash the queen of hearts and queen of clubs."

Unfavorable Lie

South's reliance on odds was wrong. Since the Universe doesn't always unfold as we would like, South must prepare for an unfavorable lie of the cards.

At the third trick, South should lead a club and play low from his hand. After ruffing the spade return, he takes the A-K of hearts before cashing the A-K of clubs and ruffing a club in dummy. This play almost assures the contract whenever hearts split 3-2.

BIDDING QUIZ

You hold: ♠ J 10 8 ♥ Q 10 3 ♦ K 10 4 ♣ Q 10 7 5. Your partner opens 1NT, and the next player passes. What do you say?

ANSWER: Bid three (count 'em, three) notrump. Even though your side may have only 24 high-card points in all, your hand is worth much more than eight points, especially for play at notrump. All four tens will be valuable, and even the eight of spades may be significant.

```
Dlr: South          ♠ A K 4 2
Vul: N-S            ♥ 7 5 2
                    ♦ 8 6 3
                    ♣ 8 6 3
♠ J 10 8                            ♠ Q 9 7 5 3
♥ Q 10 3                            ♥ J 8
♦ K 10 4                            ♦ Q J 9 5
♣ Q 10 7 5                          ♣ J 9
                    ♠ 6
                    ♥ A K 9 6 4
                    ♦ A 7 2
                    ♣ A K 4 2
```

South	West	North	East
1♥	Pass	2♥	Pass
4♥	All Pass		

Opening lead: ♠J

101.

Dlr: South   ♠ 8 7 3
Vul: N-S   ♥ K 10 4 2
        ♦ K 6 5
        ♣ 7 5 2

        ♠ K 10 5
        ♥ A Q 3
        ♦ J 8 3
        ♣ A K Q 10

South	West	North	East
1♣	Pass	1♥	Pass
2 NT	Pass	3 NT	All Pass

West leads the ♠2, and you take East's queen with the king.
When you cash the ♣AK, West discards a diamond. Both defenders follow low to the ♥AQ. Do you plan to lead a heart to
the king next or finesse with the ♥10?

102.

        ♠ 7 6
        ♥ K Q 10 3
        ♦ J 9 4
        ♣ K 10 8 6

South	West	North	East
1♣	Pass	1♥	Pass
1♠	Pass	4♠	All Pass

What should West lead?

103.

Dlr: East
Vul: N-S

    ♠ A 4 2
    ♥ K 10 4
    ♦ A 7 3
    ♣ Q 6 4 2

    ♠ K Q 5 3
    ♥ Q J 9 8 3
    ♦ K J 4
    ♣ 8

East	South	West	North
1♣	1♥	Pass	2 NT
Pass	3♣	Pass	4♥
All Pass			

West leads the ♣10, winning. You ruff the next club. How do you continue?

104.

Dlr: West
Vul: None

    ♠ 10 7 5 2
    ♥ 10 9 4
    ♦ A Q 4
    ♣ A K 5

    ♠ A K 9 8 3
    ♥ K 3
    ♦ J 7 5
    ♣ 8 7 3

West	North	East	South
1 NT	Pass	Pass	2♠
Pass	4♠	All Pass	

West leads the ♣Q. Plan the play.

101.

Unwelcome Guest

The textbook lead of the fourth-highest card helps your partner on defense. If you lead a deuce, for example, he knows you have a suit of four cards. The same information is available to declarer, however.

South won the first trick with the king of spades and cashed the A-K of clubs. When West threw a diamond, South had a proven finesse with the ten of clubs and thus needed four heart tricks to make his game. He took the ace and queen, led a third heart and put up dummy's king when West played low. East discarded, and declarer ended up down one.

Inference

South makes his game by drawing a simple inference. He knows that West had four spades (from the lead of the deuce) and one club. If West had five diamonds, he would surely lead a diamond against 3NT. South should thus play West for 4-4-4-1 distribution and finesse with the ten on the third heart lead.

I don't suggest that you abandon fourth-best leads. Just be willing to accept a good declarer as an occasional unwelcome guest at your party.

BIDDING QUIZ

You hold: ♠ K 10 5 ♥ A Q 3 ♦ J 8 3 ♣ A K Q 10. Your partner opens 1NT, and the next player (not surprisingly) passes. What do you say?

ANSWER: The textbook response is 5NT, which forces partner to bid at least 6NT and invites a grand slam. He can bid a suit at the six level to probe for a grand slam. If your partner may not have read the textbook, however, don't jeopardize your easy small slam; just bid 6NT.

Dlr: South		♠ 8 7 3	
Vul: N-S		♥ K 10 4 2	
		♦ K 6 5	
		♣ 7 5 2	
♠ A J 6 2			♠ Q 9 4
♥ J 7 6 5			♥ 9 8
♦ Q 9 7 2			♦ A 10 4
♣ 3			♣ J 9 8 6 4
		♠ K 10 5	
		♥ A Q 3	
		♦ J 8 3	
		♣ A K Q 10	

South	West	North	East
1♣	Pass	1♥	Pass
2 NT	Pass	3 NT	All Pass

Opening lead: ♠2

102.

A Killing Lead

Textbooks offer a list of desirable opening leads. The flaw in this approach is obvious: a list can't sit at the table to listen to the bidding, visualize the course of the play and pick the best lead to counter declarer's plans.

West in the deal below knew all the lists by heart; he thus started the top card in his heart sequence against South's game.

South took full advantage of this thoughtless lead. He threw a diamond on the ace of hearts, ruffed a heart, cashed the ace of clubs and ruffed a club. Next came a heart ruff, a club ruff and another heart ruff.

Tenth Trick

South then took the top diamonds and ruffed a diamond for his tenth trick. East was left to gaze forlornly at the A-K-Q of trumps.

Since West has clubs and hearts under control, and nobody bid diamonds, extra trumps are declarer's most likely source of tricks. West should therefore lead a trump and punish North for overbidding. In fact, if East is allowed to cash his high trumps on the first three tricks, South must play carefully to take even eight tricks.

BIDDING QUIZ

You hold: ♠ 7 6 ♥ K Q 10 3 ♦ J 9 4 ♣ K 10 8 6. Dealer, at your right, opens one diamond. You pass, the next player passes, and your partner bids 1NT. Opening bidder passes. What do you say?

ANSWER: When partner bids in the "passout" seat, all of his actions require less strength than usual. The 1NT bid promises 11 to 14 points, and you should therefore pass. You would raise an *opening* 1NT bid, but here, game is impossible.

```
Dlr: South          ♠ 10 8 4 3
Vul: N-S            ♥ A 9 7 4 2
                    ♦ A 10 7 3
                    ♣ None
  ♠ 7 6                              ♠ A K Q
  ♥ K Q 10 3                         ♥ J 8 6 5
  ♦ J 9 4                            ♦ Q 8 6
  ♣ K 10 8 6                         ♣ 9 7 4
                    ♠ J 9 5 2
                    ♥ None
                    ♦ K 5 2
                    ♣ A Q J 5 3 2
```

South	West	North	East
1♣	Pass	1♥	Pass
1♠	Pass	4♠ (!)	All Pass

Opening lead: ??

103.

A Simple Game

An acquaintance I know as Simple Simon likes his bridge free from complexities. "It's really a simple game," he says. "All you need to do is draw trumps and take a few finesses."

Simon, South, ruffed the second club and led a trump. East took his ace and led a trump back. My prosaic friend drew trumps and stuck to his style; he tried a finesse with the jack of diamonds, losing to the queen. When spades split 4-2, Simon also lost a spade trick and went down.

Simon's approach was too simplistic for this deal. After winning the second trump, he must abandon trumps and lead the king, ace and a low spade. If spades break 3-3, he simply draws trumps and has ten tricks.

Tenth Trick

If East ruffs in on the third spade, Simon plays low. He later discards a diamond from dummy on the queen of spades and ruffs a diamond for his tenth trick. If East doesn't ruff the third spade, Simon scores the queen and ruffs his last spade in dummy.

Actually, Simon can succeed even after he draws trumps early — but not by taking a finesse. He must ruff a third club and lead A-K-Q and a low spade. West wins and must then lead from his queen of diamonds into South's K-J.

BIDDING QUIZ

You hold: ♠ A 4 2　♥ K 10 4　♦ A 7 3　♣ Q 6 4 2. Dealer, at your right, opens one spade. What do you say?

ANSWER: Pass. It's always risky to enter an auction the opponents began. If you double, you force partner to play for eight tricks, and your support for the unbid suits is only fair. When your hand is full of losers and seems better suited to defending, be willing to wait and listen.

```
Dlr: East            ♠ A 4 2
Vul: N-S             ♥ K 10 4
                     ♦ A 7 3
                     ♣ Q 6 4 2

♠ 10 8 7 6                        ♠ J 9
♥ 5 2                             ♥ A 7 6
♦ Q 10 6 2                        ♦ 9 8 5
♣ 10 9 3                          ♣ A K J 7 5

                     ♠ K Q 5 3
                     ♥ Q J 9 8 3
                     ♦ K J 4
                     ♣ 8
```

East	South	West	North
1♣	1♥	Pass	2 NT
Pass	3♠	Pass	4♥
All Pass			

Opening lead: ♣10

104.

Gong My Way

I've never aspired to television stardom; still, I think I'd enjoy hosting a bridge edition of "The Gong Show."

Contestant South, declarer on the deal below, takes the ace of clubs at the first trick, draws trumps and wins a finesse with the queen of diamonds. He then cashes the ace of clubs and leads a third club, hoping to give West the lead.

Unfortunately, East wins the ten of clubs and leads a heart. West takes the jack and ace, and South later loses a trick to the king of diamonds. Down one.

Earns "10"

If I ran the show, South wouldn't get past the first trick; I'd gong him for winning the opening lead. South could earn a sparkling "10" from me, though, by refusing the first trick. This play prevents East from winning a club trick and sets up an endplay on West.

South wins the next club, draws trumps and finesses with the queen of diamonds. He next takes the ace of clubs and ace of diamonds and exits with a diamond.

When West wins the king, he must give South the tenth trick: a heart lead makes a winner of South's king, and a club lets South ruff in dummy and discard a heart.

BIDDING QUIZ

You hold: ♠ A K 9 8 3 ♥ K 3 ♦ J 7 5 ♣ 8 7 3. Dealer, at your left, opens one heart, and your partner doubles. The next player passes. What do you say?

ANSWER: Bid two spades. Your hand is worth a game invitation; if you bid only one spade, partner may fear you are broke. Swap your club and heart holdings and you would bid game yourself; but on your actual hand, the king of hearts, with the opening bidder sitting behind you, may be worthless.

```
Dlr: West          ♠ 10 7 5 2
Vul: None          ♥ 10 9 4
                   ♦ A Q 4
                   ♣ A K 5
♠ Q J                          ♠ 6 4
♥ A Q J 5                      ♥ 8 7 6 2
♦ K 10 6                       ♦ 9 8 3 2
♣ Q J 9 2                      ♣ 10 6 4
                   ♠ A K 9 8 3
                   ♥ K 3
                   ♦ J 7 5
                   ♣ 8 7 3
```

West	North	East	South
1 NT	Pass	Pass	2♠
Pass	4♠	All Pass	

Opening lead: ♣Q

105.

Dlr: North
Vul: N-S

```
              ♠ J 5
              ♥ A Q 4
              ♦ 10 5
              ♣ A K Q 9 6 4

        ┌─────────┐
        │    N    │        ♠ A Q 10 9 3
        │ W     E │        ♥ 10 3
        │    S    │        ♦ A J 3
        └─────────┘        ♣ 10 5 2
```

North	East	South	West
1♣	1♠	1 NT	Pass
3 NT	All Pass		

West leads the ♣8. How do you defend?

106.

Dlr: East
Vul: N-S

```
              ♠ A 6 5 2
              ♥ A J
              ♦ Q 4
              ♣ 8 7 5 4 2



              ♠ K 4 3
              ♥ K Q 10 9 8 7
              ♦ 10 6 3
              ♣ A
```

East	South	West	North
1♦	1♥	Pass	1♠
Pass	2♥	Pass	3♥
Pass	4♥	All Pass	

West leads the ♦9. East wins the jack and shifts to a trump.
Plan the play.

FRANK STEWART

107.

Dlr: South
Vul: N-S

♠ 9 7
♥ A 8 3
♦ J 10 8 4
♣ K Q 10 2

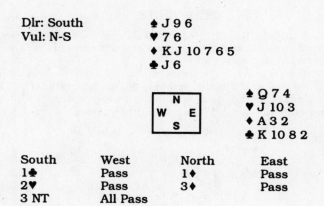

♠ J 10 5
♥ Q 10 7
♦ A 7 2
♣ 9 7 6 5

South	West	North	East
1 NT	Pass	3 NT	All Pass

West leads the ♠6: seven, ten, king. South then reaches dummy with the ♣K and leads the ♦J. How do you defend?

108.

Dlr: South
Vul: N-S

♠ J 9 6
♥ 7 6
♦ K J 10 7 6 5
♣ J 6

♠ Q 7 4
♥ J 10 3
♦ A 3 2
♣ K 10 8 2

South	West	North	East
1♣	Pass	1♦	Pass
2♥	Pass	3♦	Pass
3 NT	All Pass		

West leads the ♠2, and declarer plays the nine from dummy. Plan the defense.

105.

Be a Realist

Everybody can tell an optimist from a pessimist. (A glass is half full to one, half empty to the other.) Today's East had to be a realist, not a fatalist.

East took the ace of spades at the first trick and returned the queen. That ended the play; South won his king and claimed ten tricks.

"You defended like a masochist," West barked at partner. "Declarer has to have the king of spades. Shift to diamonds."

"I needed the ace of diamonds as an entry to my spades," East protested.

"What you need," West groaned, "is a good bridge therapist."

Finesse Wins

West was right; East's argument was sophist. After the first trick, any pragmatist can see that South has nine tricks: at least two hearts (winning a finesse if necessary), six clubs and a spade.

An artist leads the jack of diamonds at the second trick, saving the ace as an entry for a second lead through South's holding. If South covers with the queen, West wins, returns a diamond to the ace and remains with the 9-7 behind South's 8-6.

And that's the story of the deal below, as recounted by your essayist.

BIDDING QUIZ

You hold: ♠ A Q 10 9 3 ♥ 10 3 ♦ A J 3 ♣ 10 5 2. You open one spade after two passes, and your partner responds two clubs. The opponents pass. What do you say?

ANSWER: Pass. Game is impossible, especially when partner could not support spades. If you bid again, you may get too high. Clubs will be a good spot; as a passed hand, partner will avoid a temporizing response in a poor club suit, since you may drop him there.

```
Dlr: North        ♠ J 5
Vul: N-S          ♥ A Q 4
                  ♦ 10 5
                  ♣ A K Q 9 6 4
   ♠ 8 7 4                         ♠ A Q 10 9 3
   ♥ J 8 7 6 5                     ♥ 10 3
   ♦ K 9 7 2                       ♦ A J 3
   ♣ 8                             ♣ 10 5 2
                  ♠ K 6 2
                  ♥ K 9 2
                  ♦ Q 8 6 4
                  ♣ J 7 3
```

North	East	South	West
1♣	1♠	1 NT	Pass
3 NT	All Pass		

Opening lead: ♠8

106.

Avoid Speeding Train

If you see a speeding freight train headed your way, you scramble to get clear of the tracks. South in the deal below ignored the danger thundering toward him and was duly run over.

East took the jack of diamonds at the first trick and switched to a trump. South won in dummy and blithely led the queen of diamonds. East took the king and kicked declarer's caboose by leading another trump. In the end, South had to pay the freight: East got the jack of diamonds, and West got a spade trick to engineer the contract's defeat.

No Chance

If a train appears, get off the tracks; choose a line of play that has a chance, not one that is doomed to failure. South's line couldn't work unless the defense adjourned to the Pullman car for a snooze. Instead, South should play a low spade from both hands at the second trick, hoping that spades will break 3-3.

If the defenders lead another round of trumps, South draws trumps and takes the K-A of spades. Dummy's last spade then provides South with his tenth trick.

BIDDING QUIZ

You hold: ♠ J 9 7 ♥ 6 4 ♦ A K J 7 5 ♣ K Q 10. You open one diamond, and your partner bids one heart. The opponents pass. What do you say?

ANSWER: Bid 1NT, promising balanced distribution and 13 to 15 points. You don't need a sure trick in spades to make the bid that best describes your strength and pattern. A rebid of two diamonds would be wrong; it is permissible but seldom desirable to rebid a five-card suit.

```
Dlr: East              ♠ A 6 5 2
Vul: N-S               ♥ A J
                       ♦ Q 4
                       ♣ 8 7 5 4 2
  ♠ Q 10 8                             ♠ J 9 7
  ♥ 5 3 2                              ♥ 6 4
  ♦ 9 8 2                              ♦ A K J 7 5
  ♣ J 9 6 3                            ♣ K Q 10
                       ♠ K 4 3
                       ♥ K Q 10 9 8 7
                       ♦ 10 6 3
                       ♣ A
```

East	South	West	North
1♦	1♥	Pass	1♠
Pass	2♥	Pass	3♥
Pass	4♥	All Pass	

Opening lead: ♦9

107.

Higher Authority

Bridge axioms may conflict. For example, "second hand low" is good advice — unless you need to win a fast trick to "return partner's lead." When two axioms clash, try an appeal to higher authority.

South in the deal below won the king of spades at the first trick, got to dummy with a high club and led the jack of diamonds. You and I can see that East should take his ace to return a spade; otherwise, South has nine tricks (winning a finesse in hearts). How can East know to abandon "second hand low"?

Fourth Highest

To resolve the conflict, East appeals to higher authority: the good old Rule of 11. If West's spade lead is his fourth highest, East can subtract six (West's lead) from 11. The remainder, five, is the number of higher spades that East, North and South hold.

Because all five (dummy's 9-7, East's J-10 and South's king) are visible, East knows that West's spade suit is ready to cash. Since West probably has five spades (the deuce, three and four are all missing, and West will surely have the decency to hold one of them), East must grab his ace of diamonds and lead a spade.

BIDDING QUIZ

You hold: ♠ 9 7 ♥ A 8 3 ♦ J 10 8 4 ♣ K Q 10 2. Your partner opens one heart, and the next player doubles. What do you say?

ANSWER: Redouble, the usual action if you have 10 or more points. Your hand is too strong for a direct raise to two hearts. At your next turn, depending on the vulnerability, you will support hearts at the cheapest level or double the opponents for penalty if they run to a minor suit.

```
Dlr: South        ♠ 9 7
Vul: N-S          ♥ A 8 3
                  ♦ J 10 8 4
                  ♣ K Q 10 2
♠ A Q 8 6 3                        ♠ J 10 5
♥ 9 6 5 2                          ♥ Q 10 7
♦ 9 6 5                            ♦ A 7 2
♣ 8                                ♣ 9 7 6 5
                  ♠ K 4 2
                  ♥ K J 4
                  ♦ K Q 3
                  ♣ A J 4 3
```

South	West	North	East
1 NT	Pass	3 NT	All Pass

Opening lead: ♠ 6

108.

No Cover, No Minimum

The deal below was played in a nightclub bar. East-West had raised a glass or two before striking up a bridge game with the bartender and one of the showgirls.

South put up dummy's nine of spades at the first trick. He would lose a trick if West's spades were headed by K-Q, but gain if West had K-10 or Q-10 (twice as often).

South's play paid unexpected dividends when East foolishly covered with the queen of spades. South took the ace and led diamonds to force East's ace. South won the heart return, led a spade to make dummy's jack an entry and later ran the diamonds to make two overtricks.

Stone Dead

West was in no mood to buy another round of drinks. "If you don't cover the nine of spades," he told East, "we get the maximum on defense: six tricks. You wait to win the second diamond, and the dummy is stone dead. Instead, we got the minimum.

"Take a lesson from the sign outside," West finished. "'No cover, no minimum'."

West was right. East's play of the queen of spades can gain only if West has the A-K. The bidding makes that holding impossible.

BIDDING QUIZ

You hold: ♠ K 10 8 2 ♥ Q 9 8 2 ♦ 9 8 ♣ 9 4 3. Your partner opens 1NT, and the next player passes. What do you say?

ANSWER: It's tempting to bid two clubs, Stayman, but if partner lacks a major suit and bids two diamonds, you'll be stuck. If you then try 2NT, partner may bid a hopeless 3NT. To use Stayman implies game interest; thus, you must pass 1NT.

```
Dlr: South          ♠ J 9 6
Vul: N-S            ♥ 7 6
                    ♦ K J 10 7 6 5
                    ♣ J 6
♠ K 10 8 2                        ♠ Q 7 4
♥ Q 9 8 2                         ♥ J 10 3
♦ 9 8                            ♦ A 3 2
♣ 9 4 3                          ♣ K 10 8 2
                    ♠ A 5 3
                    ♥ A K 5 4
                    ♦ Q 4
                    ♣ A Q 7 5
```

South	West	North	East
1♣	Pass	1♦	Pass
2♥	Pass	3♦	Pass
3 NT	All Pass		

Opening lead: ♠2

109.

Dlr: North
Vul: N-S

♠ A 7 5 2
♥ K 4
♦ 9 6 3
♣ A K 8 4

```
        N
    W       E
        S
```

♠ Q 9 3
♥ Q 10 3
♦ Q 7
♣ Q J 9 7 2

North	East	South	West
1♣	Pass	1♥	Pass
1♠	Pass	2 NT	Pass
3 NT	All Pass		

South's jump to 2NT promises about 11 points. West leads the ♦5, and your queen wins the first trick. South takes the next diamond with the ace, and West follows with the deuce. Plan the defense from here.

110.

Dlr: South
Vul: N-S

♠ A K J
♥ 6 3
♦ J 9 8 4 2
♣ J 7 3

♠ Q 10 9 4
♥ A K
♦ Q 10 3
♣ K Q 4 2

South	West	North	East
1 NT	Pass	3 NT	All Pass

West leads the ♥Q. Plan the play.

111.

Dlr: South
Vul: N-S

      ♠ K Q 6
      ♥ K 4
      ♦ Q J 5
      ♣ 9 7 6 4 3

      ♠ A J 10 3
      ♥ A 6
      ♦ K 10 4 3
      ♣ K Q J

South	West	North	East
1 NT	Pass	3 NT	All Pass

West leads the ♥J. Plan the play (a) at rubber bridge or IMPs; (b) at matchpoint duplicate.

112.

Dlr: South
Vul: N-S

      ♠ K 9 5 2
      ♥ A 7 3
      ♦ K J 6 2
      ♣ J 8

                  ♠ 8 7
```
      N
   W     E
      S
```
                  ♥ K Q
                  ♦ A 9 5 4
                  ♣ 10 9 7 6 2

South	West	North	East
1♠	Pass	3♠	Pass
4♠	All Pass		

West leads the ♥4. Plan the defense.

109.

One Lady Too Many

East, a connoisseur of beautiful women, was charmed when he examined his hand and found a harem of four queens!

Soon the opponents bid a notrump game. (South's jump to 2NT was invitational; North's raise was a product of vulnerable greed.)

When West led a diamond, East had to release one of his lovely ladies at the first trick. South refused the first diamond, took the diamond return with his ace and, with little choice, led a heart to the king. East clutched the queen of hearts tightly to his chest, thereby handing South his contract.

Had To Win

South returned a heart to his ace and led a third heart, holding his breath. East had to win, and South was home with four heart tricks, a diamond, two spades and two clubs.

Despite his affection for the opposite sex, East must throw the queen of hearts under dummy's king. If South holds A-J-x-x-x of hearts, the queen is worth no more than a servant maid. But if West has the jack of hearts, East has a chance to create an entry to his partner's hand.

Fellow males, beware; too many fetching ladies can be your downfall.

BIDDING QUIZ

You hold: ♠ K 8 4 ♥ A 7 6 5 2 ♦ A 10 4 ♣ 5 3. Your partner opens one diamond, you respond one heart, and he rebids three diamonds. The opponents pass. What do you say?

ANSWER: Bid three spades, aiming for the nine-trick game. If partner can't bid 3NT, he may try four hearts. If he rebids four diamonds, raise to five. There is little danger he will raise spades; with four cards in spades, he'd bid one spade at his second turn.

```
Dlr: North          ♠ A 7 5 2
Vul: N-S            ♥ K 4
                    ♦ 9 6 3
                    ♣ A K 8 4
♠ J 10 6                            ♠ Q 9 3
♥ J 9 8                             ♥ Q 10 3
♦ K J 8 5 2                         ♦ Q 7
♣ 10 6                              ♣ Q J 9 7 2
                    ♠ K 8 4
                    ♥ A 7 6 5 2
                    ♦ A 10 4
                    ♣ 5 3
```

North	East	South	West
1♣	Pass	1♥	Pass
1♠	Pass	2 NT	Pass
3 NT	All Pass		

Opening lead: ♦5

110.

Where Do You Rank?

Studies conducted at the Stewart Bridge Scholastic Institute show that anyone who can make 3NT on the deal below ranks in the 98th percentile of all players.

Most Souths, when faced with the deal on the SBSI Test, win the first heart with the ace and attack diamonds, dummy's long suit. This plan fails because the opening lead has left South lagging in the race for tricks. East wins the first diamond and returns a heart, and West unblocks an honor under South's king. When West takes the next diamond, the defenders cash three hearts to beat the game.

Eight Tricks

South improves a few percentiles by attacking clubs at the second trick, but he still goes down if he leads a low club to dummy's jack. East wins and clears the hearts. When clubs split 4-2, South has only eight tricks.

Good technique will move South up to the top rank. South must get to dummy with a high spade at Trick Two and return a club toward the two honors in his hand. After the king of clubs wins, South returns to dummy to lead another club. When East's ace pops up, South is sure of three club tricks, four spades and two hearts.

BIDDING QUIZ

You hold: ♠ A K J ♥ 6 3 ♦ J 9 8 4 2 ♣ J 7 3. Your partner opens one club, you respond one diamond, and he next bids one spade. The opponents pass. What do you say?

ANSWER: To bid 1NT with two low hearts or rebid the ragged diamonds is hideous. A preference to two clubs is too discouraging and may not result in a good contract anyway. Though a raise of opener's second suit suggests four trumps, a bid of two spades is your best call.

```
       Dlr: South        ♠ A K J
       Vul: N-S          ♥ 6 3
                         ♦ J 9 8 4 2
                         ♣ J 7 3
  ♠ 7 5 2                              ♠ 8 6 3
  ♥ Q J 10 4                           ♥ 9 8 7 5 2
  ♦ A 5                                ♦ K 7 6
  ♣ 10 8 6 5                           ♣ A 9
                         ♠ Q 10 9 4
                         ♥ A K
                         ♦ Q 10 3
                         ♣ K Q 4 2
```

South	West	North	East
1 NT	Pass	3 NT	All Pass

Opening lead: ♥Q

111.

Going for Broke

At matchpoint duplicate bridge, you try to beat other pairs who hold your cards in an identical deal. In routine contracts, overtricks are therefore crucial.

South, my partner in a duplicate event, took the king of hearts and counted four spade tricks and two hearts. Since three tricks could be had in diamonds, South next led the queen of diamonds. West won the ace and led another heart. South then cashed his nine tricks and lost the rest. Making three.

Top Score

I hated to tell South he had misplayed, especially since we got a top score on the deal. Other Souths at 3NT started clubs at the second trick. East took the ace and led a heart. When clubs broke 4-1, these Souths went down.

A lucky lie of the cards saved us. Usually, clubs would break 3-2; then the other Souths would make an overtrick, while we would get a "bottom" for making only the contract.

"Silly," my partner complained, "to be punished for assuring my bid." Yet, duplicate demands high skill. A rubber-bridge player must know how to play safe; a duplicate player must also know *when* to play safe.

BIDDING QUIZ

You hold: ♠ A J 10 3 ♥ A 6 ♦ K 10 4 3 ♣ K Q J. Your partner opens one heart, you respond one spade, and he next bids 1NT. The opponents pass. What do you say?

ANSWER: Since partner promises 13 to 15 points, slam is possible. Raise to 4NT, a quantitative slam try that asks partner to look at his hand again. If he bids 6NT, you may arrive at slam with only 32 points, but your two tens should compensate.

```
Dlr: South          ♠ K Q 6
Vul: N-S            ♥ K 4
                    ♦ Q J 5
                    ♣ 9 7 6 4 3
♠ 8 5 4 2                          ♠ 9 7
♥ J 10 9 5 2                       ♥ Q 8 7 3
♦ A 9 2                            ♦ 8 7 6
♣ 2                               ♣ A 10 8 5
                    ♠ A J 10 3
                    ♥ A 6
                    ♦ K 10 4 3
                    ♣ K Q J
```

South	West	North	East
1 NT	Pass	3 NT	All Pass

Opening lead: ♥J

112.

Partner vs. Partner

Some players are more intent on winning the postmortem than the deal itself. This regrettable attitude can ruin a partnership.

South played a low heart from dummy at the first trick, and East took the queen and returned the king. South falsecarded with his jack on the second heart and won dummy's ace. He next got to his hand with a high club and led the jack of spades, faking a finesse. When West played low, South lost only a spade, a heart and a diamond, and made his game.

First Shot

East-West then played pin-the-blame-on-the-partner. East fired the first shot. "Take the ace of spades! Unless I can ruff a heart lead, we'll never beat the contract."

"If you hold the queen of spades and queen of diamonds," West countered, "we need to win two trump tricks and a diamond."

"If you take your ace," East retorted, "he may misguess in trumps anyway."

And so on.

East was at fault; he should win the *king* of hearts at the first trick and return the queen. West should grasp the significance of this unusual play and grab his ace of trumps to give East a heart ruff. The main lesson, though, is that partners should be supportive, not adversarial. Two opponents at the table are enough.

BIDDING QUIZ

You hold: ♠ 8 7 ♥ K Q ♦ A 9 5 4 ♣ 10 9 7 6 2. Your partner opens one heart, and the next player overcalls one spade. What do you say?

ANSWER: Since partner has at least five hearts, raise to two hearts. You owe him a trump, but if you don't raise, competition may shut you out forever. You can always fall back on the old plea: "I had a diamond mixed in with my hearts." (If you play negative doubles, you may prefer that action.)

```
Dlr: South          ♠ K 9 5 2
Vul: N-S            ♥ A 7 3
                    ♦ K J 6 2
                    ♣ J 8
♠ A 3                               ♠ 8 7
♥ 9 6 5 4 2                         ♥ K Q
♦ 10 8 7 3                          ♦ A 9 5 4
♣ Q 5                               ♣ 10 9 7 6 2
                    ♠ Q J 10 6 4
                    ♥ J 10 8
                    ♦ Q
                    ♣ A K 4 3
```

South	West	North	East
1♠	Pass	3♠	Pass
4♠	All Pass		

Opening lead: ♥4

113.

Dlr: East
Vul: N-S

    ♠ 8 2
    ♥ 10 8 4 2
    ♦ K J 10 5 2
    ♣ A 4

    ♠ A K 5 3
    ♥ K Q J
    ♦ Q 9 3
    ♣ Q 9 5

East	South	West	North
1♣	1 NT	Pass	3 NT
All Pass			

West leads the ♣2. Plan the play.

114.

Dlr: North
Vul: Both

    ♠ A J
    ♥ J 4
    ♦ 8 5 3
    ♣ A K J 10 5 3

♠ K Q 10 4
♥ A Q 3
♦ 9 7 4 2
♣ Q 6

```
      N
   W     E
      S
```

North	East	South	West
1♣	Pass	1♥	Pass
2♣	Pass	3♥	Pass
4♥	All Pass		

You lead the ♠K. South takes dummy's ace and leads the ♥J, losing to your queen. You cash the ♠Q, everyone following. How do you continue?

115.

Dlr: South
Vul: Both

      ♠ Q 10 3
      ♥ A 4
      ♦ 7 5
      ♣ A 9 8 5 4 2

```
        N
     W     E
        S
```

      ♠ 5
      ♥ K 10 7 3
      ♦ K 9 8 6 2
      ♣ K 7 6

South	West	North	East
1♠	Pass	2♣	Pass
3♠	Pass	4♠	Pass
6♠	All Pass		

West leads the ♣3. South wins the ace in dummy and plays the jack from his hand. Next, South draws three rounds of trumps, West following, and leads the ♣Q. West discards the ♥2. How do you defend?

116.

Dlr: North
Vul: N-S

      ♠ K J 4
      ♥ K 9 6 3
      ♦ Q 6
      ♣ A K J 9

      ♠ A 5 3 2
      ♥ A Q J 10 4
      ♦ K 4
      ♣ 10 2

North	East	South	West
1 NT	Pass	3♥	Pass
4♣	Pass	4♠	Pass
5♣	Pass	6♥	All Pass

West leads the ♦J. East takes the ace and returns a diamond. Plan the play.

113.

Deal of Doom

"Make 3NT, Flash Gordon," smirked Ming the Merciless, "and you may leave the planet Mongo with Dale Arden. Fail, and you go to the disintegrator room."

Our hero eyed the dummy, alert for insidious hidden traps. Flash was about to play a low club from dummy at the first trick when he saw that East could win the king of clubs (a card he surely held) and shift to spades. The defense might then set up two spade tricks to go with a club and East's two aces. Gordon thus rose with the ace of clubs, and Ming shook his fist with rage.

Recoils

Flash next reached for a diamond, but then recoiled. If East held three diamonds to the ace, he could refuse the first two diamond leads, holding declarer to two tricks in each suit. (Even if South shifts to hearts at the third trick, East can prevail by winning the ace and leading a low diamond!)

Flash thus led a heart at the second trick. Whatever East did, South could get three heart tricks and two tricks in each of the other suits.

"Well played, Earthman," Ming sneered. "But what about this next deal?"

Don't miss Chapter Two of "Flash Gordon Conquers the Bridge Table" on the following page!

BIDDING QUIZ

You hold: ♠ J 10 9 4 ♥ A 5 ♦ A 8 6 ♣ K J 7 3. Dealer, at your right, opens one heart, and you double. The next player jumps to three hearts, and your partner bids three spades. What do you say?

ANSWER: Pass. Your partner isn't trying for game, only competing for the partscore. Since he may have stuck his neck out to do even that, don't hang him. Your hand is minimum for a takeout double.

```
Dlr: East           ♠ 8 2
Vul: N-S            ♥ 10 8 4 2
                    ♦ K J 10 5 2
                    ♣ A 4

♠ Q 7 6                          ♠ J 10 9 4
♥ 9 7 6 3                        ♥ A 5
♦ 7 4                            ♦ A 8 6
♣ 10 8 6 2                       ♣ K J 7 3

                    ♠ A K 5 3
                    ♥ K Q J
                    ♦ Q 9 3
                    ♣ Q 9 5
```

East	South	West	North
1♣	1 NT	Pass	3 NT
All Pass			

Opening lead: ♣2

114.

Deal of Doom — 2

When we left Flash Gordon, he had just made 3NT, avoiding the fiendish traps set by Emperor Ming the Merciless. The Emperor himself then bid a game. "Set me, Earthman, and you go free," Ming hissed. "Fail, and be thrown into a bottomless pit."

Ming won the ace of spades at the first trick and led the jack of hearts for a finesse. Our hero, West, won the queen, cashed the queen of spades, and was tempted to take the ace of hearts and try for the ten of spades. He knew, however, that the crafty Ming would never play the hand this way with three low spades.

Diamond Trick

Gordon had his fingers on a fatal diamond, hoping to find East with the ace, when he realized that South's bidding promised at least 10 points; East couldn't have a fast diamond trick. Flash thus led a club.

Ming shook with rage, but he had to win and continue trumps. Flash took the ace and led the queen of clubs, severing declarer's last link with dummy. When Ming led a good club to throw his losing diamond, Gordon ruffed with his low trump to defeat the contract.

Don't miss Chapter Three of "Flash Gordon Conquers the Bridge Table" on the following page!

BIDDING QUIZ

You hold: ♠ K Q 10 4 ♥ A Q 3 ♦ 9 7 4 2 ♣ Q 6. Dealer, at your right, opens one club, you double, and your partner jumps to two spades. The opponents pass. What do you say?

ANSWER: Partner's bid invites game. He would jump with as few as nine points; otherwise, you would fear he had nothing. Since your double was minimum (subminimum, actually, since the worth of the queen of clubs is questionable), pass.

```
Dlr: North          ♠ A J
Vul: Both           ♥ J 4
                    ♦ 8 5 3
                    ♣ A K J 10 5 3
♠ K Q 10 4                              ♠ 9 7 6 5 2
♥ A Q 3                                 ♥ 6 5
♦ 9 7 4 2                               ♦ Q J 10
♣ Q 6                                   ♣ 9 7 4
                    ♠ 8 3
                    ♥ K 10 9 8 7 2
                    ♦ A K 6
                    ♣ 8 2
```

North	East	South	West
1♣	Pass	1♥	Pass
2♣	Pass	3♥	Pass
4♥	All Pass		

Opening lead: ♠K

115.

Deal of Doom — 3

When we left Flash Gordon, he was locked in a tight rubber with the Emperor Ming the Merciless. Each side had made a game when the intrepid Gordon bid a gambling slam.

West led his singleton club, and Flash escaped immediate doom by winning dummy's ace. He then drew trumps and led the queen of clubs. Ming took the king and led a diamond. Our hero won the ace, unblocked the ten of clubs, got to dummy with the ace of hearts and ran the clubs. Making six!

Confirmed

Ming's suspicions were confirmed; a heart or diamond lead would leave Gordon with no chance. In a rage, the evil emperor ordered the hapless West dragged away and fed to the giant crab monster.

"Not so fast," West snarled at Ming. "YOU can beat the slam. Lead the king of hearts when you win the king of clubs, and the Earthman must lose a diamond.

"Anybody who defends a slam that badly," West finished as he zapped Ming with a concealed ray-gun, "has no business ruling the planet Mongo." And Flash Gordon had conquered the Universe as well as the bridge table.

BIDDING QUIZ

You hold: ♠ 5 ♥ K 10 7 3 ♦ K 9 8 6 2 ♣ K 7 6. Your partner opens one spade, you bid 1NT, and he next jumps to three diamonds. The opponents pass. What do you say?

ANSWER: Partner's jump says he is confident of game now that you have responded to the opening bid. Since you have a massive diamond fit with two side kings, slam is possible. Raise to five diamonds, promising strong trumps and inviting partner to go on.

```
Dlr: South          ♠ Q 10 3
Vul: Both           ♥ A 4
                    ♦ 7 5
                    ♣ A 9 8 5 4 2
♠ 9 7 2                              ♠ 5
♥ J 9 8 5 2                          ♥ K 10 7 3
♦ Q 10 4 3                           ♦ K 9 8 6 2
♣ 3                                  ♣ K 7 6
                    ♠ A K J 8 6 4
                    ♥ Q 6
                    ♦ A J
                    ♣ Q J 10
```

South	West	North	East
1♠	Pass	2♣	Pass
3♠	Pass	4♠	Pass
6♠(!)	All Pass		

Opening lead: ♣3

116.

Do the Right Thing

"Do the right thing," North instructed his partner as they sat down to play. South promised to try.

North's bid of four clubs promised a fine hand with excellent heart support. Without help for hearts, North would always return to 3NT.

Six hearts was a good contract, but South didn't make it. East took the ace of diamonds at the first trick and returned a diamond. South won and saw a possible loser in spades. After drawing trumps, he finessed with dummy's jack of spades, and East won the queen to defeat the slam.

Club Finesse

"Would you have finessed in clubs?" South asked partner.

"Yes," North answered curtly.

"And I suppose you have a reason," South sighed.

"I always do the right thing," North replied.

North was only kidding (I hope). Still, he had the right idea. After drawing trumps, South should cash the A-K of spades. If the queen falls, South is home. If not, he still has a chance; he leads the ten of clubs to finesse and winds up shedding his last two spades. The correct play gives South two chances instead of only one.

BIDDING QUIZ

You hold: ♠ Q 9 7 ♥ 8 7 ♦ A 8 7 5 2 ♣ 8 7 4. Your partner opens one spade, and the next player bids two diamonds. What do you say?

ANSWER: Bid two spades. A penalty double suffers from two flaws: your undisclosed support for spades, and the weakness of your hand. If an opponent ran from two diamonds doubled to two hearts, your partner might double that contract unsuccessfully, expecting you to hold more strength.

```
Dlr: North          ♠ K J 4
Vul: N-S            ♥ K 9 6 3
                    ♦ Q 6
                    ♣ A K J 9
♠ 10 8 6                            ♠ Q 9 7
♥ 5 2                               ♥ 8 7
♦ J 10 9 3                          ♦ A 8 7 5 2
♣ Q 6 5 3                           ♣ 8 7 4
                    ♠ A 5 3 2
                    ♥ A Q J 10 4
                    ♦ K 4
                    ♣ 10 2
```

North	East	South	West
1 NT	Pass	3♥	Pass
4♣	Pass	4♠	Pass
5♣	Pass	6♥	All Pass

Opening lead: ♦J

117.

Dlr: South   ♠ K 6 2
Vul: N-S   ♥ K J 9 2
               ♦ J 9 6 2
               ♣ K 6

               ♠ 10
               ♥ A 5 3
               ♦ A K Q 10 5 3
               ♣ A J 4

South	West	North	East
1♦	Pass	1♥	Pass
3♣	Pass	4♦	Pass
4♥	Pass	5♣	Pass
6♦	All Pass		

West leads the ♥7. You try the nine from dummy, but East covers with the ten. Plan the play.

118.

Dlr: South   ♠ J 10 4
Vul: N-S   ♥ K 9 3
               ♦ 6 5 4 3
               ♣ A 7 5

♠ Q 6
♥ J 8 6 4   N
♦ K 9 2   W   E
♣ Q 10 8 2   S

South	West	North	East
1♠	Pass	2♠	Pass
3♠	All Pass		

You lead the ♣2. East wins the king and returns the ♣J to dummy's ace. South next leads the ♠J for a finesse, losing to your queen. Your ♣Q cashes, everyone following. How do you continue?

119.

Dlr: South
Vul: N-S

♠ J 6 4
♥ J
♦ A K Q 10 7 6
♣ 6 5 3

♠ A 10 9 2
♥ K 5 4
♦ 9 3
♣ Q 10 8 2

```
      N
  W       E
      S
```

South	West	North	East
1♥	Pass	2♦	Pass
3♣	Pass	3♦	Pass
3♥	Pass	4♥	All Pass

You lead the ♠A. East signals with the eight, and South plays the queen. How do you continue?

120.

Dlr: West
Vul: N-S

♠ K Q J 4
♥ A 4
♦ 7 4 3 2
♣ J 4 3

```
      N
  W       E
      S
```

♠ A 10 9 7
♥ 9 8
♦ J 10 9 6
♣ 9 6 2

West	North	East	South
3♥	Pass	Pass	Dbl
Pass	4♠	Pass	4 NT
Pass	5♦	Pass	6 NT
All Pass			

West leads the ♥Q. South wins in his hand with the king and leads the ♠2 to West's eight and dummy's king. How do you defend?

117.

Use Your
Opponent's Brain

Our bridge table time is split: half the time we're wrestling with our own problems; the other half we're wondering what our crafty opponents are up to. To guess what an opponent is doing, you must ask yourself what you would do in his place.

South was happy when he saw dummy; he could win 12 tricks if West had either missing heart honor or the ace of spades.

When South played dummy's nine of hearts at the first trick, East produced the ten, and South reconsidered. West would not lead from the queen of hearts when both North and South had bid hearts. West would not lead hearts at all without a good reason. The opening lead, South judged, was a sure singleton.

South still had a chance; he drew trumps and led a spade, hoping dummy's king would be winner. When East won the ace, however, South had to go down.

Places Ace

South put himself in West's shoes when he diagnosed the opening lead. He can make the slam if he also places the ace of spades.

If West is trying for a heart ruff, East must have the ace of spades. If West had an ace, he wouldn't expect East to have one and wouldn't indulge in a risky heart opening lead.

Suppose South wins the ace of hearts, draws trumps, takes the A-K of clubs, ruffs a club and runs all his trumps. With three tricks to go, dummy saves the king of spades and K-J of hearts, while South has two hearts and a spade. East must keep his ace and the Q-8 of hearts.

South then leads a spade. East must win and lead a heart into dummy's K-J to fulfill the slam.

BIDDING QUIZ

You hold: ♠ K 6 2 ♥ K J 9 2 ♦ J 9 6 2 ♣ K 6. Dealer, at your left, opens one diamond. Your partner doubles, and the next player raises to two diamonds. What do you say?

ANSWER: Since your hand is worth about 11 points, invite game with a jump to three hearts. You would bid two hearts to compete if your king of clubs were a low club.

Dlr: South
Vul: N-S

```
                      ♠ K 6 2
                      ♥ K J 9 2
                      ♦ J 9 6 2
                      ♣ K 6
♠ Q 9 8 5 4                              ♠ A J 7 3
♥ 7                                      ♥ Q 10 8 6 4
♦ 8 4                                    ♦ 7
♣ Q 10 7 5 2                             ♣ 9 8 3
                      ♠ 10
                      ♥ A 5 3
                      ♦ A K Q 10 5 3
                      ♣ A J 4
```

South	West	North	East
1♦	Pass	1♥	Pass
3♣	Pass	4♦	Pass
4♥	Pass	5♣	Pass
6♦	All Pass		

Opening lead: ♥7

118.

Big Difference

Someone asked me what single quality separates a good defender from a card pusher.

There is no easy road to becoming a demon defender. Concentration and imagination help, abundant card sense is nice, and having a good partner never hurt anyone. The essential defensive skill, though, is to distinguish the tricks you must grab quickly from the tricks that can't go away.

In the deal opposite, East takes the first club with the king and returns the jack. South wins in dummy and loses a spade finesse to West's queen. West cashes the queen of clubs, and the fate of the defense hangs on his next play.

Most Wests would know not to lead another club, which would give South a ruff-sluff, but all too many Wests would lead a red suit, hoping to find East with help. If West leads a heart, South plays low from dummy, captures East's queen and returns a heart to finesse with dummy's nine. South loses a diamond, but makes his contract, and West counts himself unlucky that East had no better than the queen in hearts.

Unlucky

If West leads a diamond, South scores the A-Q. He loses a heart, but makes his contract, and West counts himself unlucky that East had nothing good in diamonds.

West must realize that the defenders' tricks in diamonds and hearts can't go away. Dummy has few high cards and no strong suit. What losers South has, he can't avoid — unless West leads from honors in a desperate try for fast tricks.

West defeats the contract by returning a trump at the fifth trick. This play gives South nothing he can't get on his own. Say that South wins dummy's ten and finesses with the queen of diamonds. When West takes the king, the safe course is still best; West should return a diamond. South then loses a heart trick and goes down.

BIDDING QUIZ

You hold: ♠ A K 9 7 3 ♥ A 10 2 ♦ A Q ♣ 9 6 3. Your partner opens three hearts, and the next player passes. What do you say?

ANSWER: Raise to four hearts, but do no more. You might be down at the five level.

FRANK STEWART

```
Dlr: South          ♠ J 10 4
Vul: N-S            ♥ K 9 3
                    ♦ 6 5 4 3
                    ♣ A 7 5

♠ Q 6                               ♠ 8 5 2
♥ J 8 6 4                           ♥ Q 7 5
♦ K 9 2                             ♦ J 10 8 7
♣ Q 10 8 2                          ♣ K J 4

                    ♠ A K 9 7 3
                    ♥ A 10 2
                    ♦ A Q
                    ♣ 9 6 3
```

South	West	North	East
1♠	Pass	2♠	Pass
3♠	All Pass		

Opening lead: ♣2

119.

Queen at the Club

"We found this guy with a thirty-eight slug in him," Inspector Queen told Ellery, motioning to a body slumped over a nearby card table. "Name's Webb. The cards under him are the last deal he played; he must have been taking another look at it when he was plugged. We collared the other three players: Nast, Eads and Shaw."

Ellery walked over and studied the deal. "Dad, get Velie to find out the result."

The hulking Sergeant Velie soon returned. "Four hearts, making five, Maestro." He recited the auction. "Webb led the ace and ten of spades. Shaw, the declarer, ruffed, lost a trick to the king of trumps and later ran the diamonds."

Inspector Queen frowned. "With those strong diamonds in dummy," he said, "it seems like Webb would shift to a club at the second trick."

Ellery turned away. "Dad, I know who killed Webb. Get those other three players in here."

Nice Problem

"A nice problem, gentlemen," Ellery said after Shaw, Nast and Eads were herded in. "Who's the best player in the game, by the way?"

"Eads usually wins," Nast stammered.

"Eads," Ellery said, facing him, "you killed Webb. On that deal, his second spade lead gave Shaw time to draw trumps and run the diamonds. A club shift was futile; on the bidding, Shaw had to hold the A-K.

"You saw the right defense," Ellery went on. "Webb must shift to a diamond, then lead another diamond when he wins his trump trick. Shaw is cut off from dummy and has to lose two club tricks."

"Webb blew it," Eads snarled. "A diamond shift can't lose even if declarer has a singleton. Webb didn't kill the dummy, so I killed him. And I'm glad. He had it coming."

"Velie," sighed Inspector Queen, "take him away."

BIDDING QUIZ

You hold: ♠ K 8 7 5 3 ♥ 6 3 2 ♦ J 8 2 ♣ 9 4. Your partner opens 1NT, and the next player passes. What do you say?

ANSWER: With a good partner, bid two spades to sign off.

Dlr: South   ♠ J 6 4
Vul: N-S   ♥ J
                 ♦ A K Q 10 7 6
                 ♣ 6 5 3

```
♠ A 10 9 2                          ♠ K 8 7 5 3
♥ K 5 4                             ♥ 6 3 2
♦ 9 3                               ♦ J 8 2
♣ Q 10 8 2                          ♣ 9 4
```

                 ♠ Q
                 ♥ A Q 10 9 8 7
                 ♦ 5 4
                 ♣ A K J 7

South	West	North	East
1♥	Pass	2♦	Pass
3♣	Pass	3♦	Pass
3♥	Pass	4♥	All Pass

Opening lead: ♠A

120.

A Firsthand Account

When I was learning how to write about bridge deals, I was cautioned against using idioms that contained the word *hand*. If you write 'on the other hand'," my mentors warned, "readers will think you're jumping from one deal to another."

I've always kept that advice close at hand.

South in the deal opposite won the first heart with the king and led a spade to dummy's king. East took the ace, and matters were then out of his hands. South won the next heart and cashed his clubs, discarding a diamond from dummy. On the last club, East had his hands full. Whether he threw a spade or a diamond, South would get a 12th trick, and East eventually threw up his hands in disgust.

South was pleased with his handiwork. The kibitzers on hand gave him a big hand, and even East was impressed. "I have to hand it to you," he told declarer.

"Thanks for lending a hand," laughed South.

Requirements

The requirements for a squeeze go hand-in-glove: declarer needs *threat cards* with entries. He must also be one trick short of the tricks he needs; we say "the count must be rectified." East's defense was heavyhanded; he can handcuff South by refusing the first two spade leads. Since South has failed to rectify the count, he must go down.

Squeeze play requires textbook knowledge as well as hands-on experience. You might also ask a good player to take you in hand and offer a few pointers. Soon you'll be executing squeezes hand-over-fist, opponents will be eating out of your hand, and you'll be the best player in your group — hands down!

BIDDING QUIZ

You hold: ♠ 8 6 ♥ Q J 10 7 6 3 2 ♦ 8 ♣ 8 7 5. You open three hearts, the next player overcalls three spades, and your partner doubles. What do you say?

ANSWER: Pass. You told your story; now trust your partner. For all you know, he has the opponents nailed to the mast; and you might even contribute a diamond ruff.

Dlr: West   ♠ K Q J 4
Vul: N-S   ♥ A 4
                 ♦ 7 4 3 2
                 ♣ J 4 3

♠ 8 6   ♠ A 10 9 7
♥ Q J 10 7 6 3 2   ♥ 9 8
♦ 8   ♦ J 10 9 6
♣ 8 7 5   ♣ 9 6 2

                 ♠ 5 3 2
                 ♥ K 5
                 ♦ A K Q 5
                 ♣ A K Q 10

West	North	East	South
3♥	Pass	Pass	Dbl
Pass	4♠	Pass	4 NT
Pass	5♦	Pass	6 NT
All Pass			

Opening lead: ♥Q

I hope you enjoyed *Two-Minute Bridge Tips*.

This book ($11.95) and two of my other books, *My Bridge and Yours* ($11.95) and *A Christmas Stocking* ($8.00), are available directly from me, postpaid, at P. O. Box 962, Fayette AL 35555. *The Bridge Today 1001 Workbook* ($14.95 plus postage) is available from Granovetter Books, 18 Village View Bluff, Ballston Lake NY 12019. Of the rest of my books, those that remain in print are available from Baron Barclay Bridge Supply, 3600 Chamberlain Lane, Suite 230, Louisville KY 40241.

Best wishes for better bridge,

Frank Stewart